BUSINESS & MARKETING ANALYTICS

DR. REVA MISHRA

*This book is dedicated to
All MBA students*

Contents

Foreword vii

Preface ix

Acknowledgements xi

1. Introduction 1

2. Store Clustering In Retail 25

3. Chapter 3 39

4. Hr Analytics 52

5. Hr Modeling And Analytics 58

6. Digital Marketing 67

Foreword

The Author has over +15 years of professional excellence in providing Teaching, Trainings and Academic Services in different colleges of Management Completed Doctorate in Management (Ph.D) from DAVV Indore, MCA) from Rajeev Gandhi Technical University Bhopal. Master of Business Administration in Marketing Specialization, from Sikkim Manipal University, B.Sc (Computer Science) from Barkatullah University (Bhopal-M.P.) currently Associated as Research Supervisor at Pacific University Udaipur till date 3 Ph.D Research Scholars awarded Ph.D Degree Under the Guidance Currently Guiding as a Managing Editor of IJRCSM Blind Peer Reviewed International Research Journal of Computer Science and Management.(www.ijrcsm.co.in)

Working as Editorial Review Board Committee Member of KAAV International Journal and Publication. Presently associated with Indore Institute of Law as a Associate Professor/Placement Officer @ Indore Institute of Law Rank No -1Top College of MP, CG, Rajasthan

This book is specially designed for analytics professionals. It will provide detailed insights into the world of analytical knowledge and problem solving.

Preface

The first chapter sets the basic premise of the topic. It gives a basic idea of the Analytical market.

In second chapter the book discussed about Store Clustering in Retail

Thir chapter deals with Financial Analysis of the Analytics

Chapter IV deals with Human Resouces aspect of Analytics and Modeling

In its concluding chapter the bookm deals with digital marketing and Analytics

Acknowledgements

I want to give sincere thanks to my friend Mr.Deepak Anjana and Prof. Ami Agarwal and my daughter Anshika Mishra and Abeer Mishra & Special thanks to Mr. Akash Kamal Mishra for bringing out this book in a short span of time.

CHAPTER ONE

INTRODUCTION

Analytics consists of processes and technologies that enable marketers to evaluate the success and value of their marketing initiatives, identify trends and patterns over time, and make data-driven decisions.

In general, marketing analytics tools can help you achieve four goals:

- Measure campaign performance: Understand overall ROI, assess standard metrics and build more complex market mix models to maximize business impact.
- Find opportunities in marketing performance: Segment users to see who responds to which particular marketing tactic. (For example, some campaigns work better in certain regions or on mobile devices. In email marketing, you can tell who is opening your emails, see your unsubscribe rate and test subject lines.)
- Understand your customers: Mine customer demographics and behaviors, build target audiences, create statistical models to help predict campaign success.
- Understand your competition: Adjust strategy based on market research and competitive analysis.

Tracking the marketing journey

The <u>marketing funnel below</u> represents the typical B2C customer journey. The intent, of course, is for marketing to move the customer through each stage.

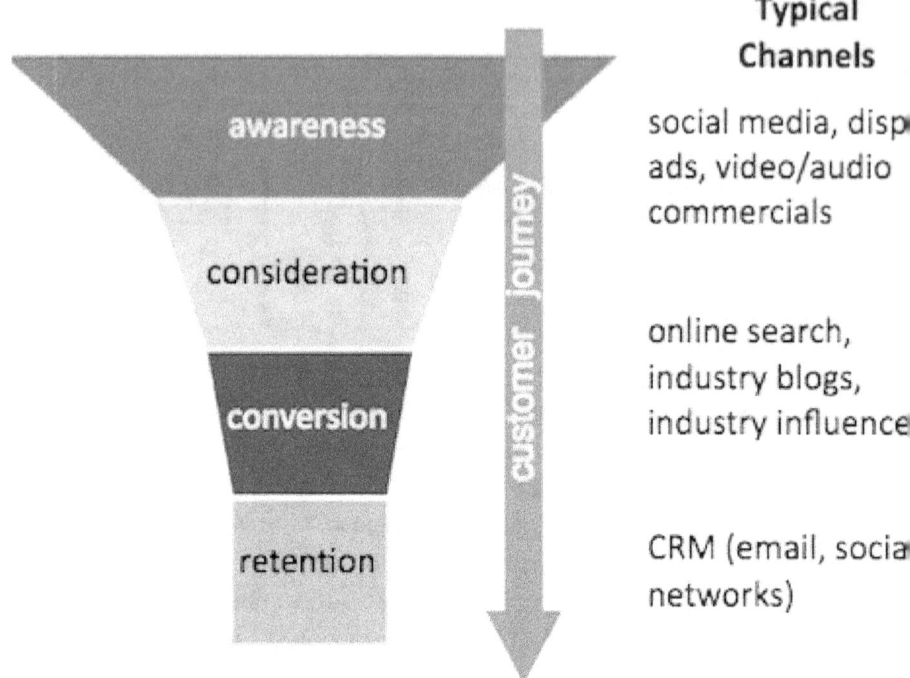

Awareness: The awareness stage is at the "top of the funnel" where you entice and educate. Campaigns, ads and content are placed where your target audience spends most of their time online. Name recognition to introduce a brand and/or product is the main goal at this stage.

Targeting is less focused. Messages should be inspirational or informative, not transactional in intent, as you're catching people early in the decision-making process. They may not need your offering right away, but are more likely to remember your message when they do. At least, they'll be primed for lower-funnel messages.

Growing your organic audience and keeping them engaged are primary goals of awareness campaigns. Marketing metrics here include reach, frequency and engagement. It isn't usually possible to accurately measure the future impact of these early campaigns. However, companies that invest in brand advertising recognize its long-term value.

Consideration/Conversion: At these next stages, buyers are more actively appraising their product choices to take action. This is where you must convince them in order to drive conversion. The message should be tailored accordingly, with a clear call to action and frictionless way to transact.

These buyers may find you through organic or paid search or via referrals, affiliates, and influencers. Marketing metrics here include sales, sign-up or other action goals. Once the transaction takes place, turn to your marketing analytics dashboard and begin to measure conversion rates of your marketing efforts.

Here is where you also capture contact information like "email address" so you can build a relationship through personalization. This leads us to the next stage.

Retention: After conversion, marketers must continue to nurture the relationship so their brands stay top of mind with their customers. An email list is a powerful asset at this stage. Email marketing analytics like click-through rates can play a big role in helping personalize retention campaigns.

All customer marketing data sources are critical to maintaining a robust customer profile. The information will inform ongoing tactics like search engine marketing, social media ads, and retargeting.

More ways to ensure data analytics in marketing success

Analytics rely on big data. For the average marketer, data may reside in over 17 different tools and applications. The key to success is being able to access combined data from multiple sources in a single place. Then, you can build strong models and clear reports.

But <u>building your own</u> data pipeline is ill-advised. The process is intensely time-consuming, error-prone and untested. Whereas an automated data integration tool like Fivetran will automatically bring all critical data together in a <u>data warehouse</u>. Then, a business intelligence tool like <u>Chartio</u> can be connected to provide intelligent visualizations, reports and dashboards.

Build meaningful marketing dashboards for your use cases

Although it's tempting to track as many metrics and KPIs as possible, <u>start</u> with a few use cases and related dashboards. Then, you can purposefully expand what you track and ensure the insights provide the most business value.

Start by defining your goals and measuring the results for the most valuable use cases. Then, try out different combinations of data to see which insights inform the best decisions. Iterating on your dashboards helps you determine the right metrics and KPIs.

Choose appropriate analytics visualizations

When building charts and dashboards, choosing the most appropriate data visualizations is important. The right view allows for accurate data interpretation and insights to action. Plus, clear reports are vital to communication marketing's value to the business.

Choose a data analytics tool that enables you to customize your visualizations instead of relying only on default charts for displaying data.

Develop models that measure and predict

Take a lesson from the Agile Methodology of continuous improvement. The approach is grounded in rapid test-and-learn cycles. In marketing, every measurement provides a new opportunity to do better — from optimizing campaigns to better customer experience and higher revenue. Try out different combinations of data to see what helps you make the best decisions.

Analyzing the past, however, is not enough in marketing. In addition to reporting campaign performance, it's important to build an analytical model that can make predictions based on customer segments.

From personal preferences and regional differences to what time of day an email should be sent or ad served, your ability to forecast will improve. And this is where the rubber meets the road in marketing — through a combination of analytics and prediction.

Conclusion

Marketing analytics measures marketing performance to improve the ROI of marketing efforts. Now that you have an overview of the goals, metrics and best practices for marketing analytics, you should have what you need to help your marketing team work more efficiently and make a bigger impact.

Marketing analytics: definition and uses

Modern marketing is a data-driven process fueled by analytics. Without analyzing relevant key performance indicators (KPI), businesses can't tell whether their marketing efforts are providing the expected return on investment (ROI). Marketing analytics is the key to evaluating past performance and determining how to improve it going forward.

What is marketing analytics?

Marketing analytics is a set of technologies and methods used to transform raw data into marketing insights. The goal of marketing analytics is to maximize ROI from an enterprise's marketing initiatives. Marketing analytics encompasses tools for planning, managing, and evaluating these efforts across every channel.

Marketers use established business metrics, and sometimes create new KPIs, to measure the success of their organizations' marketing initiatives. These metrics include:

- Profitability segmented by demographic
- Churn rate
- Customer lifetime value
- Customer satisfaction
- Public perception

Businesses can analyze performance indicators alongside other data, such as customer profiles or demographic trends, to reveal the causal links between marketing decisions and actual sales.

Try Stitch for your key data

Benefits of marketing analytics

Marketing analytics makes advertising more effective and automates many rote tasks:

- Marketing analytics helps stakeholders achieve a comprehensive view across all marketing channels, such as pay-per-click (PPC) advertising, email marketing, and social media. Analytics can clarify the big picture, as well as dig down into more granular marketing trends.
- Marketing analytics tools improve lead generation by providing the insights needed to optimize advertising efforts and target the most profitable consumers. Better leads generate more sales and improved ROI.
- Marketing analytics provides insights into customer behavior and preferences. Businesses can then tailor their marketing initiatives to meet the needs of individual consumers.
- Marketing analytics enables real-time decision support as well as proactive management. Modern analytics tools make it easy for stakeholders to analyze data as it comes in, so marketing can be adjusted as required by changing trends, and they also allow businesses to use predictive analytics to anticipate those trends rather than react to them.

Challenges of marketing analytics

Enterprises should be aware of the challenges that come with using marketing analytics:

- Many organizations and their marketing teams still struggle to integrate data, which can keep analysts and engineers from being able to access the information they need. Enterprises need to break down **data silos** that isolate information, as marketing analytics initiatives may flounder if analysts lack access to data from all marketing channels. Organizations should centralize their information in a **data warehouse** so analysts can work with integrated and accessible data.
- Enterprises need to ensure that they have management buy-in and personnel with analytics expertise. Many marketers lack analytics experience, and some executives and marketing decision-makers remain reluctant to make the up-front investments required in employees or infrastructure. Take the time up front to evaluate existing obstacles to using analytics and make the hires or **pitches** necessary to overcome them.
- Businesses need to select the right KPIs. Marketers can easily focus on metrics that are either too granular or too unfocused. To avoid this, enterprises should link performance measurements to concrete business requirements and objectives. For example, a retailer could choose a specific goal, like increasing profits by 10%, and then select a limited number of KPIs related to that goal that are appropriate for its industry, like sales per employee or average transaction value.
- Collecting any customer data involves privacy concerns. Organizations should establish **data governance** and **data security** policies to ensure that their customers' sensitive information stays protected.

How to use marketing analytics

Marketing analytics can benefit organizations' marketing initiatives across all channels. Enterprises should consider the many applications of marketing analytics and determine which may be valuable to them.

Understand search marketing

Many organizations access huge markets through search engines like Google, where consumers often begin their purchasing journeys. Search engine marketing (SEM) promotes businesses and raises online visibility through advertising on search engine results pages (SERP). Revenue from digital advertising in the U.S. breaks new records every year, and search advertising accounts for **almost half of this revenue**. Businesses can use services like Google Ads and Bing Ads to expand their reach.

Organizations need marketing analytics to track and optimize the performance of their SEM efforts. One application of SEM analytics might involve serving different versions of the same ad to a randomized set of browsers and then comparing the performance of these ads in real time.

Search engine optimization (SEO) involves adjusting web content and structure to improve organic search engine rankings. An enterprise can use SEO to reach more consumers and enhance its brand. Tools like **Google Analytics** allow businesses to track relevant KPIs and analyze how their SEO initiatives are progressing and how to improve them.

Analyze social media engagement

More than **a third of the world's population** — including **98% of digital consumers** — spend time on social media, averaging almost two and a half hours per day on these platforms. While SEM drives sales from customers who are searching for specific products, social media marketing can generate interest and demand from new groups of consumers. Social media is now the primary or sole marketing channel for many businesses and organizations, such as crafts sellers on Pinterest, fashion brands on Instagram, and nonprofits on Facebook. Many social media platforms offer their own analytics tools, such as Facebook Insights or Twitter Analytics, and third-party options are available as well.

Analyzing data obtained through social media platforms can provide valuable insights for building business or customer relationships. For example, marketers can set up an account to automatically post information about new products or features as they come out, use an analytics tool to evaluate consumer sentiment through comments or reactions without manually sifting through the data, and then rework their social media marketing as necessary.

Optimize email marketing

Though businesses can use email promotions to reach new audiences, email marketing is more often concerned with existing customers who have opted in to mailing lists or have already purchased products and services. Email provides a more direct gauge of consumer sentiment than other channels, because existing customers are more likely to respond to surveys or interact with advertised material. Popular email marketing tools include Salesforce Marketing Cloud, Mailjet, and Autopilot.

Enterprises can use analytics to optimize and personalize email marketing efforts. Analyzing how customers interact with different email promotions can help businesses target their email marketing and tailor their messages to meet customer expectations and needs. Enterprises can use marketing analytics to determine, for instance, whether customers respond well to certain keywords, emails sent at particular times of day, or links to content on specific topics.

Take advantage of predictive scoring

Predictive lead scoring models leverage marketing data from all channels, as well as internal data, to create a full picture of customer behavior, advertising potential, and marketing opportunities. These models use machine learning to build consumer profiles, which organizations can use to predict how consumers may react to different types of advertising and outreach. Campaigns can then target individual customers to maximize efficiency. For example, a predictive scoring system could rank individuals by likelihood of retention and risk of churning, which could help prioritize outreach to an organization's customer base.

Marketing analytics and the data warehouse

Enterprises should integrate their data before performing analytics, as analyzing data across marketing channels can reveal new, unexpected insights. Centralizing information in a data warehouse allows analysts and engineers to access it for analytics and reporting. Stitch provides a <u>data pipeline</u> for replicating information to the data warehouse of your choice, making it easy to integrate a wide variety of data sources.

DESCRIPTION OF CONSUMER BEHAVIOR : What is Behavioral Data?

Consumer behavior data gives insights into how consumers interact with brands and products throughout the consumer decision journey. If demographic data and other kinds of identity data help companies understand who their customers are, then consumer behavior data reveals something equally important — what they do.

As marketing becomes more sophisticated and personalized product offerings increase, companies need to know more than just who their customers are. Behavioral data gives companies new ways of understanding and segmenting consumer groups, helping companies both target the increasing number of consumers who defy demographics and identify emerging trends before they are reflected in other datasets.

A consumer behavior database is generated frequently throughout the purchase process, as consumers leave behind digital traces not only of financial transactions but of the decision-making phase that precedes these transactions, as well as the interactions with manufacturers and other consumers that occur after purchase and consumption via online reviews and social media posts. By leveraging the insights contained in this data, companies can better understand consumer preferences and product affinities and better anticipate consumer behavior, helping them make better decisions about how and when to intervene in the increasingly complex consumer decision journey.

Behavior data comes from a single-end user, an individual using a device either logged in or anonymously. Behavior datasets from various users can be collated and combined with other data to give insights into how particular types of consumers, or 'personas', behave. For example, using demographic data alongside behavior data will provide a clearer picture of how your customers interact with the business.

Consumer behavior data can be used in combination with demographic and consumer lifestyle data to help you get to know your customers as never before.

Who uses Consumer Behavior Data and for what use cases?

Consumer behavior data is used in product development, product management, marketing, data analysis, and post-sales customer service, and is vital for companies that are:

- Expanding geographically, particularly into unfamiliar markets
- Launching new products or services
- Customizing products or services for specific target markets
- Expanding their demographic reach
- Seeking to increase customer retention/loyalty

Understanding and being able to predict customer decision making, purchasing, and loyalty behavior helps companies tailor their product offerings as well as marketing and promotional activities to maximize both sales and retention.

Here of some typical uses of consumer behavior data:

Productrecommendations:

Consumer behavior insights are used to generate the recommendations that we are familiar with from online retailers and streaming services, in this case by finding patterns in purchase histories and product affinities. For example, over 80 per cent of the TV shows and movies people watch on Netflix are discovered via the platform's recommendation system. Netflix uses behavior intelligence to tailor recommendations to the user's personal interests. Amazon is also a leading user of consumer behavior data to promote products to customers based on previous purchases.

Contentoptimization:

Consumer behavior data is used to generate the recommendations that we are familiar with from online retailers and streaming services, in this case by finding patterns in purchase histories and product affinities. But you don't have to be an industry giant to leverage the up- sell and cross-sell opportunities that consumer behavior data makes possible.

For example, you might know what your customers want to buy, but when are they most likely to buy? What are the most common triggers? What kind of interactions, via which channels, typically precede a purchase? Data showing how and when customers interact with your brand — via social media, first or third party websites, mobile apps, email marketing etc. — can guide decision making about the timing and personalization of your marketing interventions to maximize sales.

Customer retention:

Companies can also use consumer behavior feeds to develop ways of reducing customer attrition or churn. Customer attrition, or churn, simply means the loss of customers. This is extremely important for a business to avoid as retaining existing customers can be much more cost-effective than acquiring new ones. In fact, it costs <u>fives times as much</u> to attract a new customer than to keep an existing one.

Companies can also use consumer behavior data to develop ways of reducing customer attrition or churn. Clearly, data on the timing and frequency of negative reviews or inbound contact with customer service can help companies predict the likelihood of customer defection and act preemptively. But consumer behavior analytics can also help uncover patterns that predict defection for the vast majority of unhappy customers who never express negative sentiment, thereby improving retention and the revenue it generates.

What other types of Consumer Data are there?

Various different kinds of data can be collected on a user which tell us more than simply how they behave. Some others include:

Basic audience data: This type of data simply tells you who your audience is. It can include contact data such as the user's name or email address, as well as demographic data about their age, gender, location and income.

Attitudinal data: Attitudinal data tells you what consumers think from their first-hand account. This is a kind of declarative data and can be obtained from the user directly by looking at surveys, online reviews or social media comments. This kind of data is useful for understanding the honest opinions of your customers, however it may not be representative of your entire audience as some consumers are more willing to share their views than others.

Interaction data: Interaction data is fairly similar to behavior data in that it shows how an audience interacts with your brand but at various stages of the consumer journey. This can include clickstream data, for example, to show how a customer arrives at a website.

Each type of data has its own advantages and disadvantages, but combining different types of data can be a useful technique for digital marketing strategies as it allows you to understand various aspects of your audience.

What are the advantages of Behavior Data?

Audience data can tell you who your audience is, such as age, location, gender, income, but this alone may not be enough to make assured business decisions. Behavior datasets tell you how your audience actually responds to content, which can give you a more accurate depiction of their choices and actions as a consumer. Drawing conclusions based on descriptive data can involve making assumptions about certain demographics, whereas behavioral insights give a much clearer picture on the actual desires of a consumer, as it is supported by evidence of their actual actions.

Behavior data intelligence is often seen as more reliable than declarative data, which is data that users give willingly themselves, as it is based on real behaviors rather than how a user considers themselves as a consumer. Declarative data such as surveys can easily be influenced by the mood or preconceptions of a consumer, whereas behavior data is true to how they actually respond and interact with the stimulus. Behavior analytics can also be more instant and can be used in real time in marketing strategies.

A survey of businesses found that, on average, 93% of businesses with an advanced personalization strategy experienced revenue growth, showing that using consumer behavior insights allows for high level personalization of content to ensure an increase in revenue.

What are typical Consumer Behavior Data attributes?

In raw form, consumer behavioral data is pretty much illegible. Lots of unstructured data and paradata is collected which needs processing in order to make sense of it. Thus, the raw data is often organized into clickstream files.

Consumer behavior data has expanded beyond its traditional reliance on the RFM model (recency, frequency, monetary spend) to encompass a variety of information collected throughout the customer decision journey. There are many different kinds of consumer behavior data at different levels of granularity. Some of the most common include:

- **Clickstream data** shows pages visited, time spent, origin, and destination

- **Loyalty program data** including join date and activity
- **Social media usage data**
- **Keywords scraped** from online reviews or social media posts
- **Product affinity data** showing which products are typically purchased together or in sequence.

What is an event?

Consumer data is usually stored in the form of an 'event'. An event refers simply to an action taken by an individual, such as clicking on a page. This data is stored alongside metadata with 'properties', which describe the event, such as the device type.

How is Behavioral Data typically collected?

Consumer Behavior Data is collected from a variety of sources, including websites, help desks, CRM systems, and mobile apps. Some of these sources — purchase information, CRM and help desk data — are internal to the company, while others are external. Traditional market research like surveys and questionnaires also yield consumer behavior datasets.

Some of the main methods of behavioral data collection include:

Cookies: Browser cookie tracking is the most common way of capturing audience data from websites and almost every website uses them. Cookies are small text files that save user-specific data in your browser. They store events such as when a user visits a site, the actions they take, the time they remain on a page and the products they buy. They reveal exactly how consumers navigate your website, which features they interact with and which they don't, and what paths lead to successful sales.

Analytics tools: Services such as Google Analytics use JavaScript code to capture data from the user's browser and count the number of page visits.

Clickstream files: As we've seen, clickstream files are a way of collecting raw behavior data and making sense of it by compiling it into a series of events which show a customer's journey through a site. Analytics tools can provide the infrastructure for this. Clickstream files include an ID to identify the individual user, an action such as the website visited, and a timestamp of when the action took place.

Market research: Surveys and questionnaires can also be used to obtain a different kind of behavioral data, declarative data. They provide an easy way to find out what your customers think about your products or services and can be of high quality since it comes directly from the user. This data provides information about brand recognition and affinity during the initial consideration and active evaluation phases, while data on how customers arrive at your digital platforms helps evaluate and focus marketing expenditures.

What is behavioral analytics?

Behavioral analytics involves looking at consumer behavioral databases to draw conclusions on the reasons for consumer actions.

Behavior analytics can be used for a variety of purposes. It is important for businesses wanting to understand their current and potential customers better and adapt their marketing strategies accordingly. It can be used in retail for product recommendations, in app and game development to predict usage trends, in social media to show recommended posts or even in political campaigns to help attract potential voters.

How to perform customer behavioral analysis?

Collect audience data: It is useful to get to know your customers with qualitative data such as demographics, location, interests. This can help to define who your audience is and which customers you should target.

1. Audience segmentation: If you have a large dataset it is hard to draw useful conclusions; this is where audience segmentation is important. Audience segmentation is the process of dividing an audience into smaller subgroups based on common characteristics, such as age, gender, location, interests, online habits. These groups can then be observed in their actions to analyze the way consumers interact with a business.

2. Acquire quantitative data: Behavior data can be collected from within the company (first party data), with usage reports and insights for example, or bought from external vendors (third-party data). By combining data from different sources you can get a good picture of how different customers behave.

3. Compare quantitative and qualitative data: Combining both data types allows you to see how different kinds of customers interact with your company in different ways. For example, which customer group buys more products, or which group returns frequently to your site.

4. Apply this information to your marketing campaign: Insights on how different types of consumers behave allow you to optimize your marketing strategy. For example, you can personalize content to target the right customers.

5. Evaluate the results: Collecting data on sales, number of website visits and revenue, for example, will help to understand if your analysis was correct and effectively used in your marketing strategy.

What types of behavioral analysis are there?

Behavioral analysis can be conducted in various ways using different tools. There are various kinds of behavioral analysis tools:

Funnel analysis: Funnel reports show a user's journey in stages, helping to visualize conversion funnels to see which consumer journeys lead to purchases and which do not. Funnels can then use testing to see what small changes can increase conversion and customer retention.

Segmentation tools: Segmentation allows you to identify KPIs and consumer trends. For example, it can be used to analyze the effectiveness of different marketing strategies by comparing the number of site visits as a result of each of them. This allows companies to identify strong and weak points in their campaigns.

Cohort analysis: Cohort analysis involves looking at specific groups of users and how they behave over time. This can be used to discover user retention rates or investigate what brings customers back for repeat purchases.

How to choose a behavioral analytics provider?

There are various programs offering behavioral data analysis, and it is important to choose the correct one for your business goals.

Some important characteristics include:

- A visualization element
- Compatibility with various systems and devices
- The ability to analyze data in different ways, so that any potential business question may be answered
- Access to data in real time
- Ability to segment data into useful data sets
- Ability to aggregate vast amounts of data
- Offering of quick results

How to assess the quality of Consumer Behavior Data?

Consumer behavior data should be targeted to your needs, up to date, and accurate. In some cases too much data can be as bad as not enough. Determining up front in consultation with a data provider what kind of data and what quantity of data will best benefit your company can save costs and frustration in the long run.

Consumers are always consuming and always generating data, so you need to ensure that your data is keeping up. Data collection is a quickly expanding industry, in fact, 90% of the world's data has been created in the last two years alone. Only data that is updated regularly — or even in real time — will help you stay on top of your markets. Frequency refers to the regularity with which data is collected, while latency measures the delay between collection and distribution. High- frequency low-latency data will keep you up to date. Data also needs to be accurate and representative in order to be relevant to your customer segments, and data providers must ensure that appropriate sampling techniques are being used to ensure accuracy.

Some things to consider when purchasing data:

- **Completeness** - are any important attributes missing? Rarity - is this data unique?
- **Usability** - how easily can the data be turned into insights? Volume - how detailed is the data?
- **Latency & frequency** - how up to date is the data? Accuracy - how accurate is the data?
- **Privacy** - does the data comply with data protection laws?

How to ensure Behavioral Data is privacy-compliant?

Behavioral data is often 'passive', i.e. consumers do not always actively participate in the collection of their data. This, however, does not mean it is collected without consent. There are various privacy laws in place such as GDPR in the EU which ensure that data collection is authorized and takes place with the permission of the user.

The General Data Protection Regulation (GDPR) was introduced in May

2018 in the EU and means it is now a requirement that consumer consent is obtained for data collection such as Cookies. This is why almost all sites ask for permission upon entering for cookie analytics to take place. The law also means that data subjects have the right to request a copy of the data or for their data to be erased. This is one of many data collection regulations which ensures transparency between consumers and customers.

How Behavioral Data is typically priced?

Consumer Behavior Data is typically sold either as a monthly subscription, which may or may not include a one-time enrollment fee, or in a single block, as with reference or historical data.

Other pricing formats are often given in CPM (cost per mille, or thousand data records), and can differ based on the geographic region covered in the data. For example, pricing may be different for EMEA (Europe, the Middle East and Africa) vs. ROW (rest of the world).

Many data providers are also willing to give out custom quotes for clients with special needs.

What are the common challenges when buying Behavioral Data?

Given the potentially unlimited scope of consumer behavior — which can include everything people do in their roles as consumers — and the vast quantities of data being generated and captured digitally, it can be difficult to know which kinds of data best suit your needs. Speaking directly to data providers is a good place to start.

Consumer behavior can also be quite volatile at times, and this volatility is reflected in the data. So it is important to make sure you're getting the right data covering both a representative audience and the right time frame, up to and including the present.

It is also important to understand where the data comes from to ensure its reliability. Research shows however, that over [50% IT leaders (57%) and IT professionals (52%)]((https://bigdata-madesimple.com/exciting-facts-and-findings-about-big-data/) report they don't always know who owns the data they use in their analytics. Not knowing the source of your data can put you at risk of making misguided marketing decisions based on inaccurate or irrelevant data.

What to ask Behavioral Data providers?

Questions you might want to ask your data provider include:

- What specific kinds of Consumer Behavior Data best suit my needs?
- How and how often is the data collected? How up to date is it?
- What format is the data supplied in, and will it work with my current enterprise software?
- Do you offer sample sets for testing purposes?
- What volume of data do you provide?

Where can I buy Consumer Behavior Data?

Data providers and vendors listed on Datarade sell Consumer Behavior Data products and samples. Popular Consumer Behavior Data products and datasets available on our platform are Consumer .

How can I get Consumer Behavior Data?

You can get Consumer Behavior Data via a range of delivery methods - the right one for you depends on your use case. For example, historical Consumer Behavior Data is usually available to download in bulk and delivered using an S3 bucket. On the other hand, if your use case is time-critical, you can buy real-time Consumer Behavior Data APIs, feeds and streams to download the most up-to-date intelligence.

What are similar data types to Consumer Behavior Data?

Consumer Behavior Data is similar to Interest Data, Consumer Lifestyle Data, Consumer Propensity Data, Consumer Intent Data, and Consumer Sentiment Data. These data categories are commonly used for advertising and Account-Based Marketing.

What are the most common use cases for Consumer Behavior Data?

The top use cases for Consumer Behavior Data are Advertising, Account-Based Marketing (ABM), and Keyword Analytics.

What are Marketing Campaigns?

Marketing campaigns are sets of strategic activities that promote a business's goal or objective. A marketing campaign could be used to promote a product, a service, or the brand as a whole. To achieve the most effective results, campaigns are carefully planned and the activities are varied. Marketing campaigns make use of different channels, platforms, and mediums to maximize impact.

A business could run campaigns that utilize print media, social media, online ads, email, in-person demos, and more. Each campaign will vary depending on the intended purpose. However, the messaging and tone of any given campaign will closely link to the tone of the business's brand. The recent increase in marketing agencies means that some businesses sometimes outsource aspects of their marketing campaigns.

How to Run a Successful Marketing Campaign

To run a successful marketing campaign, a business should take the time to plan extensively. Businesses want to be seen as proactive in their niche markets. To portray a business in a positive light or to promote products successfully, marketers need to create and execute well-researched campaign plans.

3 Types of Consumer Behavior

Why is predictive analytics important?

Organizations are turning to predictive analytics to help solve difficult problems and uncover new opportunities. Common uses include:

Detecting fraud. Combining multiple analytics methods can improve pattern detection and prevent criminal behavior. As cybersecurity becomes a growing concern, high-performance behavioral analytics examines all actions on a network in real time to spot abnormalities that may indicate fraud, zero-day vulnerabilities and advanced persistent threats.

Optimizing marketing campaigns. Predictive analytics are used to determine customer responses or purchases, as well as promote cross-sell opportunities. Predictive models help businesses attract, retain and grow their most profitable customers.

Improving operations. Many companies use predictive models to forecast inventory and manage resources. Airlines use predictive analytics to set ticket prices. Hotels try to predict the number of guests for any given night to maximize occupancy and increase revenue. Predictive analytics enables organizations to function more efficiently.

Reducing risk. Credit scores are used to assess a buyer's likelihood of default for purchases and are a well-known example of predictive analytics. A credit score is a number generated by a predictive model that incorporates all data relevant to a person's creditworthiness. Other risk-related uses include insurance claims and collections.

What Is Predictive Modeling?

In short, predictive modeling is a statistical technique using machine learning and data mining to predict and forecast likely future outcomes with the aid of historical and existing data. It works by analyzing current and historical data and projecting what it learns on a model generated to forecast likely outcomes. Predictive modeling can be used to predict just about anything, from TV ratings and a customer's next purchase to credit risks and corporate earnings.

A predictive model is not fixed; it is validated or revised regularly to incorporate changes in the underlying data. In other words, it's not a one-and-done prediction. Predictive models make assumptions based on what has happened in the past and what is happening now. If incoming, new data shows changes in what is happening now, the impact on the likely future outcome must be recalculated, too. For example, a software company could model historical sales data against marketing expenditures across multiple regions to create a model for future revenue based on the impact of the marketing spend.

Most predictive models work fast and often complete their calculations in real time. That's why banks and retailers can, for example, calculate the risk of an online mortgage or credit card application and accept or decline the request almost instantly based on that prediction.

Some predictive models are more complex, such as those used in computational biology and quantum computing; the resulting outputs take longer to compute than a credit card application but are done much more quickly than was possible in the past thanks to advances in technological capabilities, including computing power.

Top 5 Types of Predictive Models

Fortunately, predictive models don't have to be created from scratch for every application. Predictive analytics tools use a variety of vetted models and algorithms that can be applied to a wide spread of use cases.

Predictive modeling techniques have been perfected over time. As we add more data, more muscular computing, AI and machine learning and see overall advancements in analytics, we're able to do more with these models. The top five predictive analytics models are:

1. **Classification model:** Considered the simplest model, it categorizes data for simple and direct query response. An example use case would be to answer the question "Is this a fraudulent transaction?"
2. **Clustering model:** This model nests data together by common attributes. It works by grouping things or people with shared characteristics or behaviors and plans strategies for each group at a larger scale. An example is in determining credit risk for a loan applicant based on what other people in the same or a similar situation did in the past.
3. **Forecast model:** This is a very popular model, and it works on anything with a numerical value based on learning from historical data. For example, in answering how much lettuce a restaurant should order next week or how many calls a customer support agent should be able to handle per day or week, the system looks back to historical data.
4. **Outliers model:** This model works by analyzing abnormal or outlying data points. For example, a bank might use an outlier model to identify fraud by asking whether a transaction is outside of the customer's normal buying habits or whether an expense in a given category is normal or not. For example, a $1,000 credit card charge for a washer and dryer in the cardholder's preferred big box store would not be alarming, but $1,000 spent on designer clothing in a location where the customer has never charged other items might be indicative of a breached account.
5. **Time series model:** This model evaluates a sequence of data points based on time. For example, the number of stroke patients admitted to the hospital in the last four months is used to predict how many patients the hospital might expect to admit next week, next month or the rest of the year. A single metric measured and compared over time is thus more meaningful than a simple average.

What is Prescriptive Marketing?

Before we touch base on the meaning of prescriptive marketing, it's paramount to first understand the different maturity stratum of marketing analytics. They are;

Descriptive Marketing– This is the first level of marketing and in our point of view is called Data Collection phase. It has to do with Big Data. This is where data is collected and data mined from heterogeneous data ecosystems to gain insights into a customer, competitor or market. Organizations today have to pay close attention to this level of analytics because it 's the precursor to moving to next level. Emphasis should on validating and maturing your program logic to obtain a 360-degree view of data of customer data. The risk of not having good data will promote outliers and skewed data resulting inaccurate analysis.

Predictive Marketing – In this phase, the insightful information collected gets fed into built-in statistical techniques and algorithm to predict probable future outcomes of a customer based on their personas. Understanding data relationships aids in being able to segment a customer based on certain characteristics relationships. The data maturity roadmap should always be to move to a state to have deep, personalized customer understanding. Sentiment analysis is a common type of predictive analytics. That is the input to a model in plain information whereas the output to the model is a weighted score that is positive or negative or a numeral variance between +1 or -1. In this case, the model computes and is predicting the data that we don't have which is a sentiment label.

Prescriptive Marketing – This is the last stage of the maturity model of marketing analytics. In a nutshell, prescriptive marketing is a new way of thinking about customer-concentric relations utilizing the technologies of big data and machine learning which when coalesced is called Prescriptive

Marketing. Applying Prescriptive analytics is going to big game changer to organizations today because it positively impacts customer experience at every customer value-life-cycle touch points; directly boosting customers loyalties and revenues.

We believe that Prescriptive Marketing is at its infancy stage and there is allot of in tapped potential to discovering and learning more about building a personalized relationship with one's customers and marketing.

According to Inter brand, a brand's value is measured according to three core components: **The financial performance of the branded products or services. The role the brand plays in purchase decisions,The brand's competitive strength.**

CHAPTER TWO

STORE CLUSTERING IN RETAIL

What Is Financial Analysis?

Financial analysis is the process of evaluating businesses, projects, budgets, and other finance-related transactions to determine their performance and suitability. Typically, financial analysis is used to analyze whether an entity is stable, solvent, liquid, or profitable enough to warrant a monetary investment.

- If conducted internally, financial analysis can help fund managers make future business decisions or review historical trends for past successes.
- If conducted externally, financial analysis can help investors choose the best possible investment opportunities.
- Fundamental analysis and technical analysis are the two main types of financial analysis.
- Fundamental analysis uses ratios and financial statement data to determine the intrinsic value of a security.
- Technical analysis assumes a security's value is already determined by its price, and it focuses instead on trends in value over time.

Understanding data in finance : How Data Analytics Is Revolutionizing the Finance Industry

According to an article by Softweb Solutions, data analytics is revolutionizing the finance industry. One way it is accomplishing this is by reducing the component of human error from daily financial transactions.

The article lists other reasons why data analytics in finance has transformed the finance sector:

- Data analytics enables finance executives to turn structured or unstructured data into insights that promote better decision making.
- Data analytics helps finance teams gather the information needed to gain a clear view of key performance indicators (KPIs). Examples include revenue generated, net income, payroll costs, etc.
- Data analytics allows finance teams to scrutinize and comprehend vital metrics, and detect fraud in revenue turnover. This is helpful since financial services experienced a huge increase in digital fraud activity in 2020.

Additionally, big data has improved the way stock markets work and has upgraded investment-related decision making.

What Does a Finance Data Analyst Do?

Finance data analysts are professionals who help financial institutions utilize data to make high-quality business decisions. One of their primary roles is examining financial records. They do this for the purpose of preparing in-depth reports for a financial organization.

Finance data analysts often are knowledgeable of and proficient in skills related to the following topics:

- Data mining
- Financial analytics
- Understanding business models
- Financial forecasting
- Creating financial models
- Risk management
- Big data analytics
- Advanced analytics
- Data management
- Predictive analytics

- Microsoft Excel
- Algorithms and algorithmic trading
- Python
- Automation
- Data science
- Business intelligence
- Machine learning
- Artificial intelligence
- Real-time data flows

Financial analysts often work with key organizational leaders, such as chief financial officers (CFOs). They help these professionals ensure the company makes sense of its raw data and benefits from it.

The best candidates for a finance data analyst role are often junior analysts that support business functions. These functions include marketing, finance or operations roles. However, these individuals are usually asked to work closely with data to interpret and communicate what they find in the data.

By earning one or more of the best data analytics certifications, these professionals can prepare for a career in financial analysis.

The Future Role of Data Analytics in the Finance Industry

The future role of data analytics in finance is secure as data analysis is critical to the success of financial institutions. After all, as the finance sector continues to digitize, there will be more raw data for organizational leaders to interpret. Data analytics will help them make use of the data.

Amazingly, just 0.5% of businesses make use of their data, according to Data and Analytics in Financial Services. Those who practice financial data analysis can help organizations make the most of the data they collect. You can get into data analytics in finance with Comp TIA Data+ training and certification.

Get Into Finance Data Analysis with CompTIA Data+

To get your foot in the door to data analytics in finance, you'll need specialized skills. CompTIA Data+ certification training provides the skills you need to work in finance data analysis.

CompTIA Data+, which will be available in Q1 of 2022, offers a full training suite of Official CompTIA CertMaster products. These products include:

- **CertMaster Learn:** CertMaster Learn provides comprehensive eLearning that prepares you for the CompTIA Data+ certification exam.
- **CertMaster Labs:** CertMaster Labs provides hands-on experience in real virtual environments.
- **CertMaster Practice:** CertMaster Practice is an online knowledge assessment and certification exam practice and preparation companion tool.

Definition of Financial Data

Financial data consists of pieces or sets of information related to the financial health of a business. The pieces of data are used by internal management to analyze business performance and determine whether tactics and strategies must be altered.

People and organizations outside a business will also use financial data reported by the business to judge its credit worthiness, decide whether to invest in the business, and determine whether the business is complying with government regulations.

Types of Financial Data and Uses

Let's look at some of the key types of financial data that are of the most importance to internal management and outside stakeholders.

Assets include everything that a business owns and includes all personal property, real property, and intangible and tangible property. **Real property** is real estate and anything that is attached to it. **Personal property** is any property that is not real property. **Tangible property** is any physical property, such as equipment, furniture, tools, or inventory. **Intangible property** is non-physical property, such as a patent or goodwill. The total value of a company's assets is reported on the company's balance sheet.

Liabilities are the financial obligations of a company, such as what the company owes to others. Liabilities can include such things as debt, which is money owed to a lender along with any interest. Liabilities can also include accounts payable, which is money owed to suppliers for goods and services bought by the company. They also include other obligations such as wages, benefits, and taxes. Liabilities can be **short-term**, which means the obligation will come due within a year, or **long-term**, where the liability will come due in a year or longer. Liabilities are reported on the company's balance sheet.

Definition of Financial Data

Financial data consists of pieces or sets of information related to the financial health of a business. The pieces of data are used by internal management to analyze business performance and determine whether tactics and strategies must be altered.

People and organizations outside a business will also use financial data reported by the business to judge its credit worthiness, decide whether to invest in the business, and determine whether the business is complying with government regulations.

Types of Financial Data and Uses

Let's look at some of the key types of financial data that are of the most importance to internal management and outside stakeholders.

Assets include everything that a business owns and includes all personal property, real property, and intangible and tangible property. **Real property** is real estate and anything that is attached to it. **Personal property** is any property that is not real property. **Tangible property** is any physical property, such as equipment, furniture, tools, or inventory. **Intangible property** is non-physical property, such as a patent or goodwill. The total value of a company's assets is reported on the company's balance sheet.

Liabilities are the financial obligations of a company, such as what the company owes to others. Liabilities can include such things as debt, which is money owed to a lender along with any interest. Liabilities can also include accounts payable, which is money owed to suppliers for goods and services bought by the company. They also include other obligations such as wages, benefits, and taxes. Liabilities can be **short-term**, which means the obligation will come due within a year, or **long-term**, where the liability will come due in a year or longer. Liabilities are reported on the company's balance sheet.

exploratory data analysis is an approach of analyzing data sets to summarize their main characteristics, often using statistical graphics and other data visualization methods. A statistical model can be used or not, but primarily EDA is for seeing what the data can tell us beyond the formal modeling and thereby contrasts traditional hypothesis testing. Exploratory data analysis has been promoted by John Tukey since 1970 to encourage statisticians to explore the data, and possibly formulate hypotheses that could lead to new data collection and experiments. EDA is different from initial data analysis (IDA)

What is EDA(Exploratory data analysis)?

Exploratory data analysis is a great way of understanding and analyzing the data sets. The EDA technique is extensively used by data scientists and data analysts to summarize the main characteristics of data sets and to visualize them through different graphs and plots. It helps data scientists to search for patterns, spot anomalies, or check assumptions. It helps to determine if the statistical techniques that you are using for data analysis are either appropriate or not.

EDA ensures that results are valid and applicable as per the business goals. Once the EDA task is completed, its features can be used for efficient and better data analysis, modelling, and machine learning.

Investor sentiment

Investor sentiment or confidence can cause the market to go up or down, which can cause stock prices to rise or fall. The general direction that the stock market takes can affect the value of a stock:

- **bull market** – a strong stock market where stock prices are rising and investor confidence is growing. It's often tied to economic recovery or an economic boom, as well as investor optimism.
- **bear market** – a weak market where stock prices are falling and investor confidence is fading. It often happens when an economy is in recession and unemployment is high, with rising prices.

Economic factors

1. Interest rates

The <u>Bank of Canada</u> can raise or lower interest rates to stabilize or stimulate the Canadian economy. This is known as monetary policy. If a company borrows money to expand and improve its business, higher interest rates will affect the cost of its debt. This can reduce company profits and the dividends it pays shareholders. As a result, its share price may drop. And, in times of higher interest rates, investments that pay interest tend to be more attractive to investors than stocks.

2. Economic outlook

If it looks like the economy is going to expand, stock prices may rise. Investors may buy more stocks thinking they will see future profits and higher stock prices. If the economic outlook is uncertain, investors may reduce their buying or start selling.

3. Inflation

Inflation means higher consumer prices. This often slows sales and reduces profits. Higher prices will also often lead to higher interest rates. For example, the Bank of Canada may raise interest rates to slow down inflation. These changes will tend to bring down stock prices. Commodities however, may do better with inflation, so their prices may rise.

4. Deflation

Falling prices tend to mean lower profits for companies and decreased economic activity. Stock prices may go down, and investors may start selling their shares and move to fixed-income investments like <u>bonds</u>. Interest rates may be lowered to encourage people to borrow more. The goal is increased spending and economic activity. The Great Depression (1929-1939) was one of the worst periods of deflation ever.

5. Economic and political shocks

Changes around the world can affect both the economy and stock prices. For example, a rise in energy costs can lead to lower sales, lower profits and lower stock prices. An act of terrorism can also lead to a downturn in economic activity and a fall in stock prices.

6. Changes in economic policy

If a new government comes into power, it may decide to make new policies. Sometimes these changes can be seen as good for business, and sometimes not. They may lead to changes in inflation and interest rates, which in turn may affect stock prices.

7. The value of the Canadian dollar

Many Canadian companies sell products to buyers in other countries. If the Canadian dollar rises, their customers will have to spend more to buy Canadian goods. This can drive down sales, which in turn can lead to lower stock prices. When the price of the Canadian dollar falls, it makes it cheaper for others to buy our products. This can make stock prices rise.

Advertising personalization doesn't *just* include first name tokens in emails or in-app messages. With all the available data points, digital marketers should be creating personalized campaigns regularly. It's an advertising necessity.

Personalization in PPC

The amount of user data available has changed how marketers run personalization campaigns in PPC marketing, email marketing, and marketing automation. Facebook and Google, in particular, give you access to a plethora of user data such as demographics, devices, interests, behaviors, and connections to help you create personalized campaigns for every audience segment.

With PPC marketing, at the most basic level, personalized campaigns can simply refer to message matching relevant campaigns based on a user's search query or their online browsing behavior.

Message matching user queries or browsing behavior with ads and relevant post-click landing pages is one instance of PPC advertising personalization. Optimove demonstrates message match with its remarketing ad and corresponding post-click landing page below. Both feature the same (or similar) headline, copy, branding imagery, and colors:

Risk Analysis has become an integral part of every organization. There a multitude of risk analysis methods to use today. However, why do we need to perform risk analysis?

A lot of small and medium-sized businesses are facing cyber attacks. They are more at risk than larger enterprises because their security measures are often weaker. Small and medium-sized enterprises believe that their size of operations makes them less of a target. Still, cyber attackers find it a lot easier to find vulnerabilities and launch attacks on their business than the larger organizations.

A recent study stated that 78% of all participating companies in the United States survey faced a cyber attack in the last year, out of which a majority were smaller sized companies. A stable way of understanding and managing risks to companies is to invest in risk management tools and practices to protect their company's most valuable assets. Risk analysis is a big part of the risk management strategy that needs to be implemented for the risk management plan to work. The article discusses what risk analysis is and the most popular methods of conducting a risk analysis for companies.

A portfolio analysis is an interactive way of choosing the projects that offer you the best business value that can be accomplished with the people and the budget that you have available.

You might have a lot of project ideas that you want to sort through to determine what's going to give you the best business value. Or you might have a well-defined list of projects to do but not enough budget to do all of them. In either case, creating a portfolio analysis in Project Web App can help you determine which projects will give you the best business value for the budget and resources that you have available.

Business drivers

Project Web App uses business drivers that you define to help you select your projects.

A business driver is a goal that your company wants to accomplish. For example, improving customer satisfaction, expanding market share, or reducing IT costs. (It should be something really concrete that you can measure.) In Project Web App, you can define and prioritize your business drivers, and then define how each business driver is affected by a given project.

For example, a project to open a new retail store might have a strong influence on your *expand market share* business driver, but no influence on your *reduce IT costs* business driver. A project to upgrade your email system might have a strong influence on your *reduce IT costs* business driver, but none on your *improve customer satisfaction* and *expand market share* business drivers.

By defining the impact that each project or project idea has on each business driver, you give Project Web App the information that it needs to help you prioritize your projects.

What's a portfolio analysis?

Once your business drivers have been defined and prioritized, you can create a portfolio analysis.

Creating a portfolio analysis is the process of selecting a group of project ideas and, using the business drivers that you have defined, determining which are the best projects to do given your budget.

In Project Web App, you can create multiple analyses for a given set of projects and compare them to each other to help determine the best value for the budget that you have available.

hese allocations are age-based only and do not take risk tolerance into account. Our asset allocation models are designed to meet the needs of a hypothetical investor with an assumed retirement age of 65 and a withdrawal horizon of 30 years.

The model asset allocations are based upon analysis that seeks to balance long-term return potential with anticipated short-term volatility. The model reflects our view of appropriate levels of tradeoff between potential return and short-term volatility for investors of certain ages or timeframes. The longer the time frame for investing, the higher the allocation is to stocks (and the higher the volatility) versus bonds or cash.

Limitations

While the asset allocation models have been designed with reasonable assumptions and methods, the tool provides models based on the needs of hypothetical investors only and has certain limitations:

- The models do not take into account individual circumstances or preferences, and the model displayed for your investment goal and/ or age may not align with your accumulation timeframe, withdrawal horizon, or view of the appropriate levels of tradeoff between potential return and short-term volatility.

- Investing consistent with a model allocation does not protect against losses or guarantee future results.

Please be sure to take other assets, income and investments into consideration in reviewing results that do not incorporate that information. Other T. Rowe Price educational tools or advice services use different assumptions and methods and may yield different outcomes.

Credit risk analysis is **a form of analysis performed by a credit analyst on potential borrowers to determine their ability to meet debt obligations**. The main goal of credit analysis is to determine the creditworthiness of potential borrowers and their ability to honor their debt obligations.

What Is Credit Scoring?

Credit scoring is a statistical analysis performed by lenders and financial institutions to determine the credit worthiness of a person or a small, owner-operated business. Credit scoring is used by lenders to help decide whether to extend or deny credit. A credit score can impact many financial transactions, including mortgages, auto loans, credit cards, and private loans.

Bayesian methods for credit A Bayesian model is **a statistical model where you use probability to represent all uncertainty within the model, both the uncertainty regarding the output but also the uncertainty regarding the input (aka parameters) to the model**

Credit risk analytics :

What are Credit Risk Analysis Models?

Financial institutions used credit risk analysis models to determine the probability of default of a potential borrower. The models provide information on the level of a borrower's credit risk at any particular time. If the lender fails to detect the credit risk in advance, it exposes them to the risk of default and loss of funds. Lenders rely on the validation provided by credit risk analysis models to make key lending decisions on whether or not to extend credit to the borrower and the credit to be charged.

A person interested in business or finance may want to know, "What is enterprise risk analytics?" This refers to a plan or strategy for identifying everything that could possibly go wrong and affect a business's operations and objectives. This process uses data and puts the onus on the company to identify their risks and take action in order to prevent financial and figurative losses.

Identification of Risks

The identification of risk in enterprise risk analytics is usually done with a framework. There are many frameworks business managers can choose. Those include avoidance, reduction, alternative actions, sharing or insuring and acceptance. Most businesses incorporate all of these into a risk management plan. They do this after using analytical tools to identify the level of risk that each hazard presents. Some of the possible hazards to a business include property damage, natural catastrophes, intellectual property theft, liability torts, product failure, and reputation. Some other risks include social trends, internal poaching, knowledge drain, customer satisfaction, and competition.

Use of Data to Identify Risks

Companies use big data to identify risks. There are software programs that facilitate this process. A variety of data is used for the identification of risks. For example, customer satisfaction surveys, product ratings and reviews may be some inputs for customer satisfaction, reputation and product failure. Economic markers, including consumer sentiment, unemployment numbers, consumer spending, consumer confidence, inflation, and wages may also play a role in the identification of risk. Data related to the stock market, social media and website traffic for a company and its competitors also plays a role in the risk identification process.

Types of Analytical Tools for Enterprise Risk Analysis

Most of the analytical tools for enterprise risk assessment and planning are robust software packages. They include network- or server-based as well as cloud-based tools. Likelihood-Consequence or Probability-Impact, probabilistic risk assessment, and event chain methodology are a few of the processes used in analyzing risk. There are many manufacturers of proprietary software that performs one or more enterprise risk analytics. It is worth noting that interpreting the results of these analytical tools can be objective. Consumer satisfaction is one example. Some consumers only leave a review or complete a survey if they are extremely dissatisfied. It can also be difficult to tell if consumers are leaving unbiased reviews or if they are getting something in return for providing their opinions about products or services.

Benefits of Enterprise Risk Analytics

Businesses that conduct enterprise risk analytics may have an edge on their competition. When a risk presents itself, the business will have an action plan of how to respond. A business with a strong strategy on how to manage risks may find it easier to develop partnerships. According to Investopedia, enterprise risk analytics also help businesses stay in compliance with federal laws. Businesses that know what risks could affect them may have a lower risk of being affected by those risks.

Conclusion

Awareness of enterprise risk analytics could help a person make informed decisions and know more about the processes that take place in the management of companies. This knowledge also helps with understanding how to use the analytical tools and technology that drive the decisions managers make. Knowing, "What is enterprise risk analytics?" could also facilitate a person's choice of college major or career path.

What is Proactive Analytics?

Proactive analytics is an IT term that refers to taking an active approach to active business monitoring in order to prevent incidents from escalating. This involves monitoring 100% of an organization's data in real time, autonomously adjusting thresholds for and sending automatic alerts as early as possible so you can resolve problems before they negatively impact the bottom line.

Proactive analytics applies to the entire process of analysis — from data collection, all the way to insights and forecasting — and uses machine learning to achieve the speed, accuracy, and efficiency that's required in the data-rich world.

One of the core differences of proactive analytics is that it's able to automatically learn the unique behavior of each metric on its own. This key difference allows for a much greater level of granularity in the analytics process. In other words, with an autonomous analytics system you can identify issues as they happen, and proactively make changes before they dramatically impact your business.

Financial Risk Analytics program is **a conglomeration of all analytical techniques involved in Treasury, Risk and Investment Management** and this program not only focuses on core Financial Risk Analytics concepts across all types of financial risk including pricing, valuation, hedging and risk analytics across various ...

CHAPTER THREE

Understanding data in finance : How Data Analytics Is Revolutionizing the Finance Industry

According to an article by Softweb Solutions, data analytics is revolutionizing the finance industry. One way it is accomplishing this is by reducing the component of human error from daily financial transactions.

The article lists other reasons why data analytics in finance has transformed the finance sector:

- Data analytics enables finance executives to turn structured or unstructured data into insights that promote better decision making.
- Data analytics helps finance teams gather the information needed to gain a clear view of key performance indicators (KPIs). Examples include revenue generated, net income, payroll costs, etc.
- Data analytics allows finance teams to scrutinize and comprehend vital metrics, and detect fraud in revenue turnover. This is helpful since financial services experienced a huge increase in digital fraud activity in 2020.

Additionally, big data has improved the way stock markets work and has upgraded investment-related decision making.

What Does a Finance Data Analyst Do?

Finance data analysts are professionals who help financial institutions utilize data to make high-quality business decisions. One of their primary roles is examining financial records. They do this for the purpose of preparing in-depth reports for a financial organization.

Finance data analysts often are knowledgeable of and proficient in skills related to the following topics:

- Data mining
- Financial analytics
- Understanding business models
- Financial forecasting
- Creating financial models
- Risk management
- Big data analytics
- Advanced analytics
- Data management
- Predictive analytics
- Microsoft Excel

- Algorithms and algorithmic trading
- Python
- Automation
- Data science
- Business intelligence
- Machine learning
- Artificial intelligence
- Real-time data flows

Financial analysts often work with key organizational leaders, such as chief financial officers (CFOs). They help these professionals ensure the company makes sense of its raw data and benefits from it.

The best candidates for a finance data analyst role are often junior analysts that support business functions. These functions include marketing, finance or operations roles. However, these individuals are usually asked to work closely with data to interpret and communicate what they find in the data.

By earning one or more of the best data analytics certifications, these professionals can prepare for a career in financial analysis.

The Future Role of Data Analytics in the Finance Industry

The future role of data analytics in finance is secure as data analysis is critical to the success of financial institutions. After all, as the finance sector continues to digitize, there will be more raw data for organizational leaders to interpret. Data analytics will help them make use of the data.

Amazingly, just 0.5% of businesses make use of their data, according to Data and Analytics in Financial Services. Those who practice financial data analysis can help organizations make the most of the data they collect. You can get into data analytics in finance with CompTIA Data+ training and certification.

Get Into Finance Data Analysis with CompTIA Data+

To get your foot in the door to data analytics in finance, you'll need specialized skills. CompTIA Data+ certification training provides the skills you need to work in finance data analysis.

CompTIA Data+, which will be available in Q1 of 2022, offers a full training suite of Official CompTIA CertMaster products. These products include:

- **CertMaster Learn:** CertMaster Learn provides comprehensive eLearning that prepares you for the CompTIA Data+ certification exam.
- **CertMaster Labs:** CertMaster Labs provides hands-on experience in real virtual environments.
- **CertMaster Practice:** CertMaster Practice is an online knowledge assessment and certification exam practice and preparation companion tool.

Definition of Financial Data

Financial data consists of pieces or sets of information related to the financial health of a business. The pieces of data are used by internal management to analyze business performance and determine whether tactics and strategies must be altered.

People and organizations outside a business will also use financial data reported by the business to judge its credit worthiness, decide whether to invest in the business, and determine whether the business is complying with government regulations.

Types of Financial Data and Uses

Let's look at some of the key types of financial data that are of the most importance to internal management and outside stakeholders.

Assets include everything that a business owns and includes all personal property, real property, and intangible and tangible property. **Real property** is real estate and anything that is attached to it. **Personal property** is any property that is not real property. **Tangible property** is any physical property, such as equipment, furniture, tools, or inventory. **Intangible property** is non-physical property, such as a patent or goodwill. The total value of a company's assets is reported on the company's balance sheet.

Liabilities are the financial obligations of a company, such as what the company owes to others. Liabilities can include such things as debt, which is money owed to a lender along with any interest. Liabilities can also include accounts payable, which is money owed to suppliers for goods and services bought by the company. They also include other obligations such as wages, benefits, and taxes. Liabilities can be **short-term**, which means the obligation will come due within a year, or **long-term**, where the liability will come due in a year or longer. Liabilities are reported on the company's balance sheet.

Definition of Financial Data

Financial data consists of pieces or sets of information related to the financial health of a business. The pieces of data are used by internal management to analyze business performance and determine whether tactics and strategies must be altered.

People and organizations outside a business will also use financial data reported by the business to judge its credit worthiness, decide whether to invest in the business, and determine whether the business is complying with government regulations.

Types of Financial Data and Uses

Let's look at some of the key types of financial data that are of the most importance to internal management and outside stakeholders.

Assets include everything that a business owns and includes all personal property, real property, and intangible and tangible property. **Real property** is real estate and anything that is attached to it. **Personal property** is any property that is not real property. **Tangible property** is any physical property, such as equipment, furniture, tools, or inventory. **Intangible property** is non-physical property, such as a patent or goodwill. The total value of a company's assets is reported on the company's balance sheet.

Liabilities are the financial obligations of a company, such as what the company owes to others. Liabilities can include such things as debt, which is money owed to a lender along with any interest. Liabilities can also include accounts payable, which is money owed to suppliers for goods and services bought by the company. They also include other obligations such as wages, benefits, and taxes. Liabilities can be **short-term**, which means the obligation will come due within a year, or **long-term**, where the liability will come due in a year or longer. Liabilities are reported on the company's balance sheet.

exploratory data analysis is an approach of analyzingdata sets to summarize their main characteristics, often using statistical graphics and other data visualization methods. A statistical model can be used or not, but primarily EDA is for seeing what the data can tell us beyond the formal modeling and thereby contrasts traditional hypothesis testing. Exploratory data analysis has been promoted by John Tukey since 1970 to encourage statisticians to explore the data, and possibly formulate hypotheses that could lead to new data collection and experiments. EDA is different from initial data analysis (IDA)

What is EDA(Exploratory data analysis)?

Exploratory data analysis is a great way of understanding and analyzing the data sets. The EDA technique is extensively used by data scientists and data analysts to summarize the main characteristics of data sets and to visualize them through different graphs and plots. It helps data scientists to search for patterns, spot anomalies, or check assumptions. It helps to determine if the statistical techniques that you are using for data analysis are either appropriate or not.

EDA ensures that results are valid and applicable as per the business goals. Once the EDA task is completed, its features can be used for efficient and better data analysis, modelling, and machine learning.

Investor sentiment

Investor sentiment or confidence can cause the market to go up or down, which can cause stock prices to rise or fall. The general direction that the stock market takes can affect the value of a stock:

- **bull market** – a strong stock market where stock prices are rising and investor confidence is growing. It's often tied to economic recovery or an economic boom, as well as investor optimism.
- **bear market** – a weak market where stock prices are falling and investor confidence is fading. It often happens when an economy is in recession and unemployment is high, with rising prices.

Economic factors

1. Interest rates

The Bank of Canada can raise or lower interest rates to stabilize or stimulate the Canadian economy. This is known as monetary policy. If a company borrows money to expand and improve its business, higher interest rates will affect the cost of its debt. This can reduce company profits and the dividends it pays shareholders. As a result, its share price may drop. And, in times of higher interest rates, investments that pay interest tend to be more attractive to investors than stocks.

2. Economic outlook

If it looks like the economy is going to expand, stock prices may rise. Investors may buy more stocks thinking they will see future profits and higher stock prices. If the economic outlook is uncertain, investors may reduce their buying or start selling.

3. Inflation

Inflation means higher consumer prices. This often slows sales and reduces profits. Higher prices will also often lead to higher interest rates. For example, the Bank of Canada may raise interest rates to slow down inflation. These changes will tend to bring down stock prices. Commodities however, may do better with inflation, so their prices may rise.

4. Deflation

Falling prices tend to mean lower profits for companies and decreased economic activity. Stock prices may go down, and investors may start selling their shares and move to fixed-income investments like bonds. Interest rates may be lowered to encourage people to borrow more. The goal is increased spending and economic activity. The Great Depression (1929-1939) was one of the worst periods of deflation ever.

5. Economic and political shocks

Changes around the world can affect both the economy and stock prices. For example, a rise in energy costs can lead to lower sales, lower profits and lower stock prices. An act of terrorism can also lead to a downturn in economic activity and a fall in stock prices.

6. Changes in economic policy

If a new government comes into power, it may decide to make new policies. Sometimes these changes can be seen as good for business, and sometimes not. They may lead to changes in inflation and interest rates, which in turn may affect stock prices.

7. The value of the Canadian dollar

Many Canadian companies sell products to buyers in other countries. If the Canadian dollar rises, their customers will have to spend more to buy Canadian goods. This can drive down sales, which in turn can lead to lower stock prices. When the price of the Canadian dollar falls, it makes it cheaper for others to buy our products. This can make stock prices rise.

Advertising personalization doesn't *just* include first name tokens in emails or in-app messages. With all the available data points, digital marketers should be creating personalized campaigns regularly. It's an advertising necessity.

Personalization in PPC

The amount of user data available has changed how marketers run personalization campaigns in PPC marketing, email marketing, and marketing automation. Facebook and Google, in particular, give you access to a plethora of user data such as demographics, devices, interests, behaviors, and connections to help you create personalized campaigns for every audience segment.

With PPC marketing, at the most basic level, personalized campaigns can simply refer to message matching relevant campaigns based on a user's search query or their online browsing behavior.

Message matching user queries or browsing behavior with ads and relevant post-click landing pages is one instance of PPC advertising personalization. Optimove demonstrates message match with its remarketing ad and corresponding post-click landing page below. Both feature the same (or similar) headline, copy, branding imagery, and colors:

Risk Analysis has become an integral part of every organization. There a multitude of risk analysis methods to use today. However, why do we need to perform risk analysis?

A lot of small and medium-sized businesses are facing cyber attacks. They are more at risk than larger enterprises because their security measures are often weaker. Small and medium-sized enterprises believe that their size of operations makes them less of a target. Still, cyber attackers find it a lot easier to find vulnerabilities and launch attacks on their business than the larger organizations.

A recent study stated that 78% of all participating companies in the United States survey faced a cyber attack in the last year, out of which a majority were smaller sized companies. A stable way of understanding and managing risks to companies is to invest in risk management tools and practices to protect their company's most valuable assets. Risk analysis is a big part of the risk management strategy that needs to be implemented for the risk management plan to work. The article discusses what risk analysis is and the most popular methods of conducting a risk analysis for companies.

A portfolio analysis is an interactive way of choosing the projects that offer you the best business value that can be accomplished with the people and the budget that you have available.

You might have a lot of project ideas that you want to sort through to determine what's going to give you the best business value. Or you might have a well-defined list of projects to do but not enough budget to do all of them. In either case, creating a portfolio analysis in Project Web App can help you determine which projects will give you the best business value for the budget and resources that you have available.

Business drivers

Project Web App uses business drivers that you define to help you select your projects.

A business driver is a goal that your company wants to accomplish. For example, improving customer satisfaction, expanding market share, or reducing IT costs. (It should be something really concrete that you can measure.) In Project Web App, you can define and prioritize your business drivers, and then define how each business driver is affected by a given project.

For example, a project to open a new retail store might have a strong influence on your *expand market share* business driver, but no influence on your *reduce IT costs* business driver. A project to upgrade your email system might have a strong influence on your *reduce IT costs* business driver, but none on your *improve customer satisfaction* and *expand market share* business drivers.

By defining the impact that each project or project idea has on each business driver, you give Project Web App the information that it needs to help you prioritize your projects.

What's a portfolio analysis?

Once your business drivers have been defined and prioritized, you can create a portfolio analysis.

Creating a portfolio analysis is the process of selecting a group of project ideas and, using the business drivers that you have defined, determining which are the best projects to do given your budget.

In Project Web App, you can create multiple analyses for a given set of projects and compare them to each other to help determine the best value for the budget that you have available.

hese allocations are age-based only and do not take risk tolerance into account. Our asset allocation models are designed to meet the needs of a hypothetical investor with an assumed retirement age of 65 and a withdrawal horizon of 30 years.

The model asset allocations are based upon analysis that seeks to balance long-term return potential with anticipated short-term volatility. The model reflects our view of appropriate levels of tradeoff between potential return and short-term volatility for investors of certain ages or timeframes. The longer the time frame for investing, the higher the allocation is to stocks (and the higher the volatility) versus bonds or cash.

Limitations -

While the asset allocation models have been designed with reasonable assumptions and methods, the tool provides models based on the needs of hypothetical investors only and has certain limitations:

- The models do not take into account individual circumstances or preferences, and the model displayed for your investment goal and/ or age may not align with your accumulation timeframe, withdrawal horizon, or view of the appropriate levels of tradeoff between potential return and short-term volatility.
- Investing consistent with a model allocation does not protect against losses or guarantee future results.

Please be sure to take other assets, income and investments into consideration in reviewing results that do not incorporate that information. Other T. Rowe Price educational tools or advice services use different assumptions and methods and may yield different outcomes.

Credit risk analysis is **a form of analysis performed by a credit analyst on potential borrowers to determine their ability to meet debt obligations**. The main goal of credit analysis is to determine the creditworthiness of potential borrowers and their ability to honor their debt obligations.

What Is Credit Scoring?

Credit scoring is a statistical analysis performed by lenders and financial institutions to determine the creditworthiness of a person or a small, owner-operated business. Credit scoring is used by lenders to help decide whether to extend or deny credit. A credit score can impact many financial transactions, including mortgages, auto loans, credit cards, and private loans.

Bayesian methods for credit A Bayesian model is **a statistical model where you use probability to represent all uncertainty within the model, both the uncertainty regarding the output but also the uncertainty regarding the input (aka parameters) to the model**

Credit risk analytics :

What are Credit Risk Analysis Models?

Financial institutions used credit risk analysis models to determine the probability of default of a potential borrower. The models provide information on the level of a borrower's credit risk at any particular time. If the lender fails to detect the credit risk in advance, it exposes them to the risk of default and loss of funds. Lenders rely on the validation provided by credit risk analysis models to make key lending decisions on whether or not to extend credit to the borrower and the credit to be charged.

A person interested in business or finance may want to know, "What is enterprise risk analytics?" This refers to a plan or strategy for identifying everything that could possibly go wrong and affect a business's operations and objectives. This process uses data and puts the onus on the company to identify their risks and take action in order to prevent financial and figurative losses.

Identification of Risks

The identification of risk in enterprise risk analytics is usually done with a framework. There are many frameworks business managers can choose. Those include avoidance, reduction, alternative actions, sharing or insuring and acceptance. Most businesses incorporate all of these into a risk management plan. They do this after using analytical tools to identify the level of risk that each hazard presents. Some of the possible hazards to a business include property damage, natural catastrophes, intellectual property theft, liability torts, product failure, and reputation. Some other risks include social trends, internal poaching, knowledge drain, customer satisfaction, and competition.

Use of Data to Identify Risks

Companies use big data to identify risks. There are software programs that facilitate this process. A variety of data is used for the identification of risks. For example, customer satisfaction surveys, product ratings and reviews may be some inputs for customer satisfaction, reputation and product failure. Economic markers, including consumer sentiment, unemployment numbers, consumer spending, consumer confidence, inflation, and wages may also play a role in the identification of risk. Data related to the stock market, social media and website traffic for a company and its competitors also plays a role in the risk identification process.

Types of Analytical Tools for Enterprise Risk Analysis

Most of the analytical tools for enterprise risk assessment and planning are robust software packages. They include network- or server-based as well as cloud-based tools. Likelihood-Consequence or Probability-Impact, probabilistic risk assessment, and event chain methodology are a few of the processes used in analyzing risk. There are many manufacturers of proprietary software that performs one or more enterprise risk analytics. It is worth noting that interpreting the results of these analytical tools can be objective. Consumer satisfaction is one example. Some consumers only leave a review or complete a survey if they are extremely dissatisfied. It can also be difficult to tell if consumers are leaving unbiased reviews or if they are getting something in return for providing their opinions about products or services.

Benefits of Enterprise Risk Analytics

Businesses that conduct enterprise risk analytics may have an edge on their competition. When a risk presents itself, the business will have an action plan of how to respond. A business with a strong strategy on how to manage risks may find it easier to develop partnerships. According to <u>Investopedia</u>, enterprise risk analytics also help businesses stay in compliance with federal laws. Businesses that know what risks could affect them may have a lower risk of being affected by those risks.

Conclusion

Awareness of enterprise risk analytics could help a person make informed decisions and know more about the processes that take place in the management of companies. This knowledge also helps with understanding how to use the analytical tools and technology that drive the decisions managers make. Knowing, "What is enterprise risk analytics?" could also facilitate a person's choice of college major or career path.

What is Proactive Analytics?

Proactive analytics is an IT term that refers to taking an active approach to active business monitoring in order to prevent incidents from escalating. This involves monitoring 100% of an organization's data in real time, autonomously adjusting thresholds for and sending automatic alerts as early as possible so you can resolve problems before they negatively impact the bottom line.

Proactive analytics applies to the entire process of analysis — from data collection, all the way to insights and forecasting — and uses machine learning to achieve the speed, accuracy, and efficiency that's required in the data-rich world.

One of the core differences of proactive analytics is that it's able to automatically learn the unique behavior of each metric on its own. This key difference allows for a much greater level of granularity in the analytics process. In other words, with an autonomous analytics system you can identify issues as they happen, and proactively make changes before they dramatically impact your business.

Financial Risk Analytics program is **a conglomeration of all analytical techniques involved in Treasury, Risk and Investment Management** and this program not only focuses on core Financial Risk Analytics concepts across all types of financial risk including pricing, valuation, hedging and risk analytics across various ...

CHAPTER FOUR

HR ANALYTICS

What Is HR Analytics? Definition, Importance, Key Metrics, Data Requirements, and Implementation

Human resources is a people-oriented function and is so perceived by most people. But for those who think that the HR team's contributions are limited to extending offer letters and onboarding new hires, human resource analytics (HR analytics) can prove them wrong. When used strategically, analytics can transform how HR operates, giving the team insights and allowing it to actively and meaningfully contribute to the organization's bottom line.

What Is HR Analytics?

To understand the essence of HR analytics and to explain how it impacts business performance, we asked Mick Collins, Global Vice President, Workforce Analytics & Planning Solution Strategy and Chief Expert at SAP SuccessFactors, to break it down for us.

"HR analytics is a methodology for creating insights on how investments in human capital assets contribute to the success of four principal outcomes: (a) generating revenue, (b) minimizing expenses, (c) mitigating risks, and (d) executing strategic plans. This is done by applying statistical methods to integrated HR, talent management, financial, and operational data," says Collins in an exclusive discussion with HR Technologist.

HR analytics: HR analytics specifically deals with the metrics of the HR function, such as time to hire, training expense per employee, and time until promotion. All these metrics are managed exclusively by HR for HR.

People analytics: People analytics, though comfortably used as a synonym for HR analytics, is technically applicable to "people" in general. It can encompass any group of individuals even outside the organization. For instance, the term "people analytics" may be applied to analytics about the customers of an organization and not necessarily only employees.

Predictive analytics is an upcoming trend in Human Resources (HR). Recruitment tools predict high performers, and increasingly companies are able to predict which employee is likely to leave. In this article, we will explain what HR predictive analytics are and how they can be a real game-changer for HR departments.

The logic behind HR predictive analytics

Do you know what your personal credit score, the Oakland Athletics baseball team manager Billy Bean from the movie Moneyball and your Match.com profile have in common? They all combine big data and predictive analytics in order to predict the future.

Predictive data analytics are everywhere. It is in its essence a technology that learns from existing data, and it uses this to forecast individual behavior. This means that predictions are very specific. In the movie Money ball, predictive analytics were used to predict the potential success of individual baseball players.

Business applications for HR analytics: When it comes to building a successful business, arguably the most valuable asset is the people within the organization. Human resource management departments are increasingly looking to data analytics to inform their key people decisions, and thanks to evolving artificial intelligence and machine learning, HR professionals now have even more data available to help inform these decisions. While tech-driven intelligence and data analytics **plays a critical part in the hiring process** for many organizations, a growing number are applying increasingly sophisticated HR metrics to make data-driven people decisions that will impact employees throughout their career journey within the organization. As **Deloitte reported** in 2017, 71% of companies said they considered people analytics a high priority for their organization with 31% rating it "very important."

Areas that used to be determined solely through human feedback and review, including promotions, salary rates, attrition and retention, and training and development, are now increasingly data-driven decisions informed by artificial intelligence-powered analytics. A key value differentiator of these AI-derived metrics is that they can be gathered and analyzed in real time to help support in-the moment decisions.

Here are five ways HR and talent management teams are applying data analytics to cultivate employee development and create **high-performing organizations.**

Measuring Performance

Organizations can use analytics tools to establish employee performance benchmarks, and then coach existing and incoming employees to understand those qualities and their impact. <u>Deloitte</u>, along with other companies, analyzes human performance data, travel data and billing hours, to help individuals boost their professional performance as well as their wellness and energy. Organizations can even use data gathered from top-performing teams or individual employees as a means to understanding effective processes and set standard benchmarks for other groups in the organization to follow.

Informing Promotion and Salary Decisions

A major demotivator for many high-performing employees is watching under-performing peers receive promotions. There can be several factors that lead to this, but human bias and nepotism can often play a part. **Taking a data-based approach** can help organizational leaders watch the rate at which employees are receiving promotions and raises and what key factors drive these decisions. For example, a new employee may have just delivered an outstanding sales performance, but a longer-tenured peer may have consistently provided quality performance over time. Which performance metric carries more weight, and over what timeframe is performance measured? Should tenure be a factor at all? Gathering and using more types and sources of data and using it to train **artificial intelligence algorithms** can then support managers in making less-biased decisions and ensure performance-generated data is a larger part of the equation.

Understanding Attrition and Increasing Retention

Performance-based analytics can also be applied to predict which employees might be more prone to leave, while also telling a story about what factors contribute to attrition. Money may be less of a factor than the quality of managers and supervisors, according to management consulting firm **McKinsey & Co.** For example, McKinsey cites a case study of a major U.S. insurance company that implemented a bonus program in an effort to retain employees but saw little success. Then, the company began to apply data analytics to understand at-risk workers, and they uncovered a trend: people who were on smaller teams, went longer between promotions, and who reported to lower-performing managers were all more likely to leave. Instead of pouring money into these employees, the company began pouring resources into making stronger managers.

Organizations can also glean data on their turnover rate (both voluntary and involuntary attrition divided by average headcount) to understand trends and address sudden spikes. For example, a surge in involuntary attrition may be an indication the recruiting and training process needs a review; an uptick in voluntary attrition may require deeper dives into specific departments or managers.

Examining Employee Engagement

A crucial metric for any HR department is employee engagement. This data is typically gathered via employee engagement surveys that are conducted by outsourced survey providers (i.e. Gallup). However, more organizations are seeing the benefit of bringing this in house to their HR departments for both faster results and to maintain the ownership of their employees' data. Instead of the extensive surveys that many employees dread (and some don't even fill out), in house HR departments can use brief, small surveys to regularly monitor engagement, and with the help of **AI tools**, gain immediate data insights.

Another tool that is both an additional source of employee data and improved engagement is gamification. GamEffective, a company that designs **gamification apps** for businesses, offers one version where employees can place bets about how their day will go, based off their goals for the day. This can increase not only the employee's engagement but also motivate the employee to meet their individual and team goals, as organizations can pick specific KPIs to measure within the app.

Measuring Employee Development and Learning Outcomes

A vibrant training program can benefit organizations with a more productive workforce and improved retention. Rather than ask employees a few static questions at the completion of training, organizations can shift focus from satisfaction with the training to comprehension of the program, tracking the employee's actual progress throughout the training. Companies can go one step further by applying predictive analytics to customize training content that better meets employee learning styles at an individual level. At an organizational level, predictive analytics can assess weak points in the training (like when employee engagement dips). Ultimately, this data can analyze patterns that make a training successful and direct companies to improve content in the right places.

Turning Data Analytics into People Analytics

While these intelligent data metrics certainly give HR professionals valuable knowledge, it's crucial for HR to continue to maintain the human element of their role to ensure these tools truly add human value. One way is using the analytics behind these five applications to inform organizational design through predictive strategy that can help guide the specifications of future positions, help prepare workers to up their skill sets for these roles and meet the organization's needs.

With roughly <u>40% of companies</u> worldwide automating their HR departments, a data-rich HR department needs professionals who are adept in the analytical competencies to interpret and harness the power behind data-driven intelligence. Expanding skills and knowledge in data mining and management, machine learning applications and business analytics can provide HR professionals (and their organizations) a competitive advantage.

What is HR analytics?

HR analytics is a data-driven approach to managing people at work. HR analytics, also known as people analytics, workforce analytics, or talent analytics, revolves around analyzing people problems using data to answer critical questions about your organization. This enables better and data-driven decision-making.

What are common data sources for HR analytics?

Common data sources include internal data like demographic employee data, payroll data, social network data, performance data, and engagement data. External data sources can include labor market data, population data, LinkedIn data, and much more. Any data that's relevant for the specific project can be used.

What skills are required to do people analytics?

Relevant skills for people analytics include business consulting to identify critical issues, analytical skills to run the analysis, stakeholder management to bring everyone together and enable the people analytics project, and storytelling and visualization in order to communicate effectively with the business and share results.

HR analytics and Hr Strategy : What is HR analytics?

HR analytics is a data-driven approach to managing people at work. HR analytics, also known as people analytics, workforce analytics, or talent analytics, revolves around analyzing people problems using data to answer critical questions about your organization. This enables better and data-driven decision-making.

What are common data sources for HR analytics?

Common data sources include internal data like demographic employee data, payroll data, social network data, performance data, and engagement data. External data sources can include labor market data, population data, LinkedIn data, and much more. Any data that's relevant for the specific project can be used.

What skills are required to do people analytics?

Relevant skills for people analytics include business consulting to identify critical issues, analytical skills to run the analysis, stakeholder management to bring everyone together and enable the people analytics project, and storytelling and visualization in order to communicate effectively with the business and share results.

CHAPTER FIVE

HR Modeling and Analytics

HR Modeling Human Resources models help to explain the role of HR in the business. In this article, we will go over the 5 most practical HR models. These models enable us to explain what HR's role is, how HR adds value to the business, and how the business .

The diversity, equity and inclusion (DE&I) function deals with the qualities, experiences and work styles that make individuals unique (e.g., age, race, religion, disabilities, ethnicity) as well as how organizations can leverage those qualities in support of business objectives. It also includes matters that focus on diversity-related careers, communications, legal and regulatory issues, technology, metrics, outsourcing, effective diversity practices, and global diversity issues. It touches on but does not primarily deal with federal, state and local equal employment opportunity (EEO) laws. These are encompassed under the EEO topic within both the staffing management function (for EEO matters arising in the pre-employment context) and the employee relations function (for EEO matters arising within the employer-employee relationship.

Studies show that teams or organizations made up of individuals with a diverse mix of qualities, experiences and work styles tend to have available a richer set of ideas, perspectives and approaches to a business issue. *See 6 Steps for Building an Inclusive Workplace.*

This overview covers the following major topics:

- Relationship with equal employment opportunity and affirmative action.
- The business case for DE&I.
- Designing a DE&I initiative.

- Elements of a DE&I initiative.
- Diversity recruitment and sourcing.
- Change management as it relates to diversity, equity and inclusion.
- Careers in diversity.

DIVERSITY

Diversity has many definitions. Organizations frequently adapt the definition to their specific environment. Generally, diversity refers to the similarities and differences among individuals accounting for all aspects of their personality and individual identity. Some of the common dimensions of diversity are shown below, with a sampling of related content:

- Age. *See* How Attracting and Retaining Older Employees Can Help Your Business.
- Disability. *See* How can HR help introduce more people with disabilities into the workforce?
- Ethnicity/national origin. *See* Asian Americans Face Violence, Workplace Discrimination.
- Family status.
- Sex. *See* Bridging the Gender Divide.
- Gender identity or expression. *See* Employing Transgender Workers.
- Generation. *See* Harnessing the Power of a Multigenerational Workforce.
- Language. *See* Viewpoint: The Silencing of ESL Speakers.
- Life experiences. *See* Viewpoint: The Forgotten Dimension of Diversity
- Neurodiversity. *See* How to Attract and Support Neurodiverse Talent.
- Organizational function and level.
- Physical characteristics.
- Race/color. *See* More Racial Diversity at Tech Companies Can Help Eliminate Biased Products.
- Religion, belief and spirituality. *See* Prayer and Meditation Rooms Can Increase Inclusion.
- Sexual orientation.
- Veteran status. *See* Building and Sustaining a Veteran-Informed Culture: A Guide for HR Professionals.

INCLUSION

"Diversity is being invited to the party. Inclusion is being asked to dance." —Vernā Myers

Diversity provides the *potential* for greater innovation and creativity.Inclusionis what enables organizations to *realize the business benefits* of this potential.

Inclusion describes the extent to which each person in an organization feels welcomed, respected, supported and valued as a team member. Inclusion is a two-way accountability; each person must grant and accept inclusion from others. In such an environment, every employee tends to feel more engaged and is more likely to contribute to the organization's business results. This type of environment requires people from diverse backgrounds to communicate and work together, and to understand one another's needs and perspectives—in other words, to demonstrate cultural competence. *See* Inclusion: Out of the Training Room and into Employees' Hands and Want a Diverse and Inclusive Workplace? Work on Your Culture.

EQUITY

Equity in the workplace refers to fair treatment in access, opportunity and advancement for all individuals. Work in this area includes identifying and working to eliminate barriers to fair treatment for disadvantaged groups, from the team level through systemic changes in organizations and industries. Effecting change through an equity lens generally requires an understanding that the societal systems in which we currently work are not equitable and that those inequities are reflected in our organizations.

See:

Do Your Employees Know Why You Believe in Racial Equity?

How to Ensure Pay Equity for People of Color

Barriers for Black Professionals

INTERCULTURAL SENSITIVITY

Intercultural sensitivity andcultural (or intercultural) competenceare characterized by sensitivity to differences among people from different cultural backgrounds and effectiveness in communicating and working with them. People are similar or different in varying degrees across all dimensions of diversity. Research shows that people who are substantially alike tend to more easily communicate with and understand one another. People who are very different tend to confront more obstacles to effective communication and mutual understanding. Research also shows that people consistently overestimate their intercultural competence, which poses a particular challenge for employers. *See* Effective Workplace Conversations on Diversity.

Relationship with Equal Employment Opportunity and Affirmative Action

There is widespread confusion about the relationship between diversity and inclusion on the one hand, and EEO and affirmative actionon the other. This traces to the historical evolution of these complementary yet distinct concepts. In the United States, EEO concerns fairness and equality of treatment for specifically designated protected classes as defined by law. EEO means that the employer gives equal consideration both in hiring and in the terms and conditions of employment to all individuals, and that the employer does not discriminate on the basis of race, color, religion, age, marital status, national origin, disability or sex (including sexual orientation and gender identity or expression).

Affirmative action plans are requirements for certain federal contractors and subcontractors to take affirmative action to ensure that all individuals have an equal opportunity for employment, without regard to race, color, religion, sex (including sexual orientation and gender identity or expression), national origin, disability or status as a Vietnam era or special disabled veteran.

EEO and affirmative action are primarily matters of legal compliance, although they do help create a workplace that is more supportive of all people and more diverse in terms of the specifically included dimensions of diversity.

Many early diversity programs grew out of a company's EEO and affirmative action programs. Companies began seeing the business opportunity in focusing on awareness and sensitivity training, and later in building inclusion and intercultural competence. But the diversity functional area has evolved well beyond EEO and affirmative action compliance. DE&I is aimed at realizing competitive advantage and business opportunity.

The interrelationship among EEO, affirmative action, and DE&I persists, in part because some organizational structures place functional accountability for the disciplines under one office. Though this interrelationship can lead to some continuing confusion, progress in each of these areas reinforces and helps achieve the objectives of the others.

See What is the difference between EEO, affirmative action and diversity?

The Business Case for Diversity

Thebusiness casefor diversity is an organization's statement of purpose in working on DE&I. There are many valid reasons for doing such work. The most effective reasons for any organization are aligned directly with that organization's key business objectives. Typically, these are the business objectives on which organizations measure and compensate their senior leadership's performance. In for-profit companies, these objectives relate to factors like sales, market share, profitability, corporate social responsibility and reputation. *See* Diversity Drives Better Business Outcomes: A Q&A with Sonia Aranza.

BUSINESS CASE SELF-ASSESSMENT

- Who are your organization's key internal and external stakeholders whose needs and concerns must be considered by your diversity business case?
- What are your organization's key business objectives that the diversity business case must directly support?
- What changes are needed in your workforce to help ensure that your organization can meet its key business objectives?
- What changes are needed in your workplace (i.e., how people work together) to help ensure that your organization can meet its key business objectives?
- What changes are needed in your products and services, or in how they are produced, to help ensure that your organization can meet its key business objectives?

BUSINESS CASE ACTION STEPS

- Obtain agreement with your CEO and senior management team about the key stakeholders and key business objectives.
- Define the changes needed in the areas considered during the business self-assessment. Focus specifically on changes needed to achieve the agreed-upon key business goals.
- Assess the current situation versus the changes defined in the step above to characterize the "gap."
- Define initiatives to close the gap. Measure the extent to which the changes are put in place.
- If your organization is global in nature, do not be satisfied with input strictly from corporate headquarters; rather, seek the counsel of all key

world geographies represented in your organization.

See Report: Most Companies Are 'Going Through the Motions' of DE&I.
Design of a DE&I Initiative

Effective diversity initiativesrequire starting, planning, speaking and acting solely from key business priorities. The design and implementation process should adhere to these principles:

- Engage the CEO, senior leadership and other key stakeholders throughout the process.
- Focus on achieving business results.
- Start from, and stay aligned with, the business purpose.
- Be grounded in ownership and accountability.
- Plan ongoing internal and external communication to inform, engage and manage expectations.

If a diversity initiative is well-designed, it should be able to explain the:

- Key business priorities the initiative will help meet.
- Changes in the workforce that are needed to help meet business priorities.
- Changes in the work environment that are needed to help meet business priorities.
- Elements of a diversity initiative that will be put in place to achieve the needed changes.

The design process should address two additional areas—metrics and diversity training. Metrics can be designed once the needed changes are identified. Training may be designed to close specific gaps that are subsequently recognized. Both are integral parts of the overall initiative. *See* HR Tech's Expanded Role in Supporting DE&I Initiatives and Does Diversity Training Work the Way It's Supposed To?

ELEMENTS OF A DE& INITIATIVE

A DE&I initiative is an organization's formal strategic plan for addressing diversity and inclusion. *See* How to Develop a Diversity, Equity and Inclusion Initiative.

Effective initiatives tend to exhibit several characteristics. For example, they:

- Align with the organization's key business objectives.
- Focus on implementing specific changes to the workforce and workplace that will help a
- Identify the organization's level of intercultural competence and capacity to accept cultural change.
- Use a strategic and ongoing approach to employee communication.

Predictive modeling for training Predictive modeling is a mathematical process used to predict future events or outcomes by analyzing patterns in a given set of input data. It is a crucial component of predictive analytics, a type of data analytics which uses current and historical data to forecast activity, behavior and trends. In short, predictive modeling is a statistical technique using machine learning and data mining to predict and forecast likely future outcomes with the aid of historical and existing data. It works by analyzing current and historical data and projecting what it learns on a model generated to forecast likely outcomes. What Is Predictive Modeling?

In short, predictive modeling is a statistical technique using machine learning and data mining to predict and forecast likely future outcomes with the aid of historical and existing data. It works by analyzing current and historical data and projecting what it learns on a model generated to forecast likely outcomes. Predictive modeling can be used to predict just about anything, from TV ratings and a customer's next purchase to credit risks and corporate earnings.

A predictive model is not fixed; it is validated or revised regularly to incorporate changes in the underlying data. In other words, it's not a one-and-done prediction. Predictive models make assumptions based on what has happened in the past and what is happening now. If incoming, new data shows changes in what is happening now, the impact on the likely future outcome must be recalculated, too. For example, a software company could model historical sales data against marketing expenditures across multiple regions to create a model for future revenue based on the impact of the marketing spend.

Most predictive models work fast and often complete their calculations in real time. That's why banks and retailers can, for example, calculate the risk of an online mortgage or credit card application and accept or decline the request almost instantly based on that prediction.

Some predictive models are more complex, such as those used in computational biology and quantum computing; the resulting outputs take longer to compute than a credit card application but are done much more quickly than was possible in the past thanks to advances in technological capabilities, including computing

Top 5 Types of Predictive Models

Fortunately, predictive models don't have to be created from scratch for every application. Predictive analytics tools use a variety of vetted models and algorithms that can be applied to a wide spread of use cases.

Predictive modeling techniques have been perfected over time. As we add more data, more muscular computing, AI and machine learning and see overall advancements in analytics, we're able to do more with these models.

The top five predictive analytics models are:

1. **Classification model:** Considered the simplest model, it categorizes data for simple and direct query response. An example use case would be to answer the question "Is this a fraudulent transaction?"
2. **Clustering model:** This model nests data together by common attributes. It works by grouping things or people with shared characteristics or behaviors and plans strategies for each group at a larger scale. An example is in determining credit risk for a loan applicant based on what other people in the same or a similar situation did in the past.
3. **Forecast model:** This is a very popular model, and it works on anything with a numerical value based on learning from historical data. For example, in answering how much lettuce a restaurant should order next week or how many calls a customer support agent should be able to handle per day or week, the system looks back to historical data.
4. **Outliers model:** This model works by analyzing abnormal or outlying data points. For example, a bank might use an outlier model to identify fraud by asking whether a transaction is outside of the customer's normal buying habits or whether an expense in a given category is normal or not. For example, a $1,000 credit card charge for a washer and dryer in the cardholder's preferred big box store would not be alarming, but $1,000 spent on designer clothing in a location where the customer has never charged other items might be indicative of a breached account.
5. **Time series model:** This model evaluates a sequence of data points based on time. For example, the number of stroke patients admitted to the hospital in the last four months is used to predict how many patients

the hospital might expect to admit next week, next month or the rest of the year. A single metric measured and compared over time is thus more meaningful than a simple average.

The logic behind HR predictive analytics

Do you know what your personal credit score, the Oakland Athletics baseball team manager Billy Bean from the movie Moneyball and your Match.com profile have in common? They all combine big data and predictive analytics in order to predict the future.

Predictive data analytics are everywhere. It is in its essence a technology that learns from existing data, and it uses this to forecast individual behavior. This means that predictions are very specific. In the movie Money ball, predictive analytics were used to predict the potential success of individual baseball players.

The logic behind HR predictive analytics

Do you know what your personal credit score, the Oakland Athletics baseball team manager Billy Bean from the movie Moneyball and your Match.com profile have in common? They all combine big data and predictive analytics in order to predict the future.

Predictive data analytics are everywhere. It is in its essence a technology that learns from existing data, and it uses this to forecast individual behavior. This means that predictions are very specific. In the movie Moneyball, predictive analytics were used to predict the potential success of individual baseball players.

Predictive analytics in practice

Say there is a playground next to your house. For the past two weeks, you wrote down if there were kids playing on the playground or not. You also wrote down if it was sunny, rainy or cloudy, the temperature and the humidity. Based on the data you collected, would you be able to predict if kids will be playing on the playground on a specific day.

CHAPTER SIX

DIGITAL MARKETING

What is web analytics?

Web analytics is the measurement and analysis of data to inform an understanding of user behavior across web pages.

Analytics platforms measure activity and behavior on a website, for example: how many users visit, how long they stay, how many pages they visit, which pages they visit, and whether they arrive by following a link or not.

Businesses use web analytics platforms to measure and benchmark site performance and to look at key performance indicators that drive their business, such as purchase conversion rate.

Why web analytics are important?

There's an old business adage that whatever is worth doing is worth measuring.

Website analytics provide insights and data that can be used to create a better user experience for website visitors.

Understanding customer behavior is also key to optimizing a website for key conversion metrics.

For example, web analytics will show you the most popular pages on your website, and the most popular paths to purchase.

With website analytics, you can also accurately track the effectiveness of your online marketing campaigns to help inform future efforts.

Sample web analytics data

Web analytics data is typically presented in dashboards that can be customized by user persona, date range, and other attributes. Data is broken down into categories, such as:

Audience data

- number of visits, number of unique visitors
- new vs. returning visitor ratio
- what country they are from
- what browser or device they are on (desktop vs. mobile)

Audience behavior

- common landing pages
- common exit page
- frequently visited pages
- length of time spent per visit
- number of pages per visit
- bounce rate

Campaign data

- which campaigns drove the most traffic
- which websites referred the most traffic
- which keyword searches resulted in a visit
- campaign medium breakdown, such as email vs. social media

Web analytics examples

The most popular web analytics tool is Google Analytics, although there are many others on the market offering specialized information such as real-time activity or heat mapping.

The following are some of the most commonly used tools:

- Google Analytics - the 'standard' website analytics tool, free and widely used
- Piwik - an open-source solution similar in functionality to Google and a popular alternative, allowing companies full ownership and control of their data

- Adobe Analytics - highly customizable analytics platform (Adobe bought analytics leader Omniture in 2009)
- Kissmetrics - can zero in on individual behavior, i.e. cohort analysis, conversion and retention at the segment or individual level
- Mixpanel - advanced mobile and web analytics that measure actions rather than pageviews
- Parse.ly - offers detailed real-time analytics, specifically for publishers
- CrazyEgg - measures which parts of the page are getting the most attention using 'heat mapping'

How web analytics work

Most analytics tools 'tag' their web pages by inserting a snippet of JavaScript in the web page's code.

Using this tag, the analytics tool counts each time the page gets a visitor or a click on a link. The tag can also gather other information like device, browser and geographic location (via IP address).

Web analytics services may also use cookies to track individual sessions and to determine repeat visits from the same browser.

Since some users delete cookies, and browsers have various restrictions around code snippets, no analytics platform can claim full accuracy of their data and different tools sometimes produce slightly different results. op Benefits of Social Media Marketing for Small Businesses

In the past few years, not only has social media shown tremendous and dream-like growth but also successfully pervaded the online consciousness of all internet users worldwide. Today its influence is even more widespread, and its footprints are impossible to ignore in commercial and business circles. Social media marketing has become so important and vital, that businesses are increasingly planning and strategizing on it to optimally exploit it to their business's profitability. Here we list the top benefits of social media marketing for business for all those skeptics who are yet to see its viability.

Increases Brand Awareness

Owing to its huge user database, social media is a highly effective and extremely low-cost means to increase brand awareness and generate new customers. It can easily create familiarity with your company's web presence and leaves an imprint on the minds of customers, prospects, and patrons. Most social accounts allow free registration and only demand your time. However, an account should be properly utilized and well maintained, and you should be active and vigilant enough to develop maximum connections. Brand awareness not only positively influences the buying patterns and behaviors of the customers but also further cements the loyalty of customers.

Legitimizes Your Brand

Customers tend to conduct an online search about a brand quite regularly. If the same information is made available on social media, it goes a long way toward customer recognition of a company's product and services, leading to brand legitimization.

Increases Website Traffic and SEO Ranking

Over 80% of marketers claim that increased social media presence culminates in increased website traffic. This is hardly surprising, given the fact that over 73% of adults who remain online spend a great deal of time on social media like Facebook, Twitter, LinkedIn, etc. Facebook is the top social website that attracts the largest amount of traffic. Additionally, it has been established that the higher the number of media shares received by you, the higher your ranking in search engines.

Lead Generation Happens at Minimum Costs

The cost per lead generation from social media amounts to about just about a fraction of the cost per lead through traditional means like newspapers, radio, or commercials. It is believed that it can save up to about 80% of the total lead generation costs, which assists in increasing the company's ROI, both by cost-cutting and increased sales. Moreover, social networks also have the availability of cost-effective paid advertising options like Facebook Ads and Twitter Ads, which allow any business establishment to scale, increase reach, and fuel demand generation. Considering that lead generation is the oxygen of any business process, doing so at a minimal cost can only be profitable and advantageous.

Boosts Content Marketing

To attribute greater emphasis on content, even search engines like Google have recently changed their search engine algorithms. Even though content marketing emerges as the most important digital marketing tool of 2015, as per the digital marketing trends poll, it remains a sore area for any marketer to disseminate the content to maximum customers in the shortest time. Social media goes a long way in addressing the issue. Sharing content on your business has become quite easier and faster through various social media platforms. Nevertheless, while sharing content on social platforms, you need to ensure that the social content not only aligns with your brand but also whets the customer's interest and attention.

Brings About an Increase in Sales

As more and more people engage with your brand and follow it, more and more successful opportunities for sales will ensue. The increased number of likes, sharing, or recommendations of content happens on various social platforms and leads to increased sales. More often than not, the contents are embedded with sales and marketing elements, which facilitate sales.

Provides You with a Better Audience Insight

Social media makes it easy for any company to know its audience and reach out to them. Through various tools, one can easily learn the dominant language spoken, age, gender, interests, etc. This assists you in designing campaigns and making relevant product offers, thereby giving you a better return on investment.

There is a myth that social media can only assist big companies, and not small businesses and startups, and this discourages them from making use of it effectively. Any business can benefit from knowing its customers and connecting with them on social media. It is even more beneficial for the smaller companies, as they have less money to invest in marketing and advertising. Wondering which of your social media tactics are working? Want to better focus your time, effort, and budget? You need a social media analytics tool.

In this article, we'll cover some of **the best free social media analytics tools** available, along with some paid options (for the true nerds who want to dive deep on the data and see real returns).

Then you'll be ready to learn which social media metrics are important to track.

Not ready to start looking for at analytics tools? Get a primer on what social media analytics even is.

10 of the best social media analytics tools

Social media analytics tool #1: Hootsuite Analytics

Social media analytics tool #2: Google Analytics

Social media analytics tool #3: UTM parameters

Social media analytics tool #4: Hootsuite Insights powered by Brandwatch

Social media analytics tool #5: Brandwatch

Social media analytics tool #6: Talkwalker

Social media analytics tool #7: Hootsuite Impact

Social media analytics tool #8: Channelview Insights

Social media analytics tool #9: Mentionlytics

Social media analytics tool #10: Panoramiq Insights

Why you need social media analytics tools

Social media analytics tools help you create performance reports to share with your team, stakeholders, and boss — to figure out what's working and what's *not*. They should also provide the data you need to assess your social media marketing strategy on both macro and micro levels.

They can help you answer questions like:

- Is it worth it for my business to keep posting on Pinterest?
- What were our top posts on LinkedIn this year?
- Should we post more on Instagram next month?
- Which network drove the most brand awareness for our product launch?
- What kind of posts do my followers like to comment on?
- And many more.

10 of the best social media analytics tools

Social media analytics tool #1: Hootsuite Analytics

Key benefits: Performance data from every social network in one place with easy-to-understand reports. Social posts metrics:

- Clicks
- Comments
- Reach
- Engagement rate
- Impressions
- Shares
- Saves
- Video views
- Video reach
- And more

Profile metrics:

- Follower growth over time
- Negative feedback rate
- Profile visits
- Reactions
- Overall engagement rate
- And more

Best time to post recommendations:

Ever spend a bunch of time writing and designing a social post only to have it fall completely flat? There could be a lot of reasons for that. But one of the most common reasons this happens is *posting at the wrong time.* A.k.a. Posting when your target audiences are not online or not interested in engaging with you.

This is why our **Best Time to Publish tool** is one of the most popular features of Hootsuite Analytics. It looks at your unique historical social media data and recommends the most optimal times to post based on three different goals:

1. Engagement

2. Impressions
3. Link clicks

Why you need Google Analytics

Google Analytics is a robust and powerful tool that provides indispensable information about your website and visitors.

With more than 56% of all websites using Google Analytics, it's also one of the most popular tools out there for digital marketers — and for good reason. The tool allows you to access a wealth of information regarding your site's visitors.

Here's just a few pieces of data you can get from Google Analytics:

- Amount of traffic your site gets overall
- The websites your traffic came from
- Individual page traffic
- Amount of leads converted
- The websites your leads came form
- Demographic information of visitors (e.g. where they live)
- Whether your traffic comes from mobile or desktop

It doesn't matter if you're a freelancer with a humble blog or if you're a big company with a massive website. Anyone can benefit from the information in Google Analytics.

Now that you know how great it is, let's jump into exactly how to set up Google Analytics for your own website.

How to set up Google Analytics in 5 simple steps

Setting up Google Analytics can be tricky. However, once you have it set up, you stand to gain a ton of invaluable information very quickly.

This is pure 80/20 — with a small amount of work now you stand to gain disproportionate rewards later.

To set up Google Analytics, you simply have to follow these steps:

- Step 1: Set up Google Tag Manager
- Step 2: Create Google Analytics account

- Step 3: Set up analytics tag with Google Tag Manager
- Step 4: Set up goals
- Step 5: Link to Google Search Console

Let's jump in.

Step 1: Set up Google Tag Manager

Google Tag Manager is a free tag management system from Google.

The way it works is simple: Google Tag Manager takes all the data on your website and sends it to other platforms such as Facebook Analytics and Google Analytics.

It also allows you to easily update and add tags to your Google Analytics code without having to manually write code on the back end—saving you time and a lot of headaches down the road.

14 key metrics in Google Analytics for digital marketing

As almost anyone who runs a website knows, Google Analytics provides insight into who site visitors are and what they do when they come to a website. Marketers use Google Analytics to understand the effects of marketing campaigns and how a site's user experience impacts factors such as conversion and retention.

The **hundreds of metrics and dimensions** available in Google Analytics may seem daunting. We've zeroed in on 14 essential metrics for marketers, how to find them in the Google Analytics dashboard and via the API, and how marketers can use them to make data-driven business decisions.

Google Analytics for marketers

The Google Analytics dashboard is organized in four sections:

- **Audience** helps you explore *who* your customers are, including information such as demographics, location, retention, and device technology. With these metrics, you can interpret the impact of your marketing efforts on various user segments.
- **Acquisition** shows you *how* customer get to your website. In the Channels section under All Traffic, you can dig into what channels

(organic traffic, social media, email, ads, etc.) deliver the most traffic. You can compare incoming visitors from Facebook versus Instagram, determine the efficacy of your SEO efforts on organic search traffic, and see how well your email campaigns are running.

- **Behavior** explains *what* customers do on your website. What pages do they visit? How long do they stay? You can examine these metrics to understand the overall user experience and its effects on retention and engagement.
- **Conversions** tracks whether customers take actions that you *want* them to take. This typically involves defining funnels for important actions — such as purchases — to see how well the site encourages these actions over time.

Google Analytics separates data into dimensions and metrics. Dimensions are categorical attributes, such as the city where a user is located or the browser they use, while metrics are the quantitative measurements, such as number of sessions or pages per session. According to Google, "Not every metric can be combined with every dimension. Each dimension and metric has a scope: user-level, session-level, or hit-level. In most cases, it only makes sense to combine dimensions and metrics that share the same scope." For a list of valid dimension-metric pairs, use the Dimensions and Metrics Reference.

Search Traffic Campaigns

Overview

Users arrive at your website or application through a variety of sources, including advertising campaigns, search engines, and social networks. This article describes how Analytics collects, processes, and reports the campaign and traffic-source data.

If you're experiencing unexpected fluctuations or inconsistencies in your traffic, use this troubleshooter to identify and resolve the issues.

Understanding campaigns & traffic sources

In Analytics, the ad campaigns, search engines, social networks, and other sources that send users to your property are collectively known as campaigns and traffic sources. The process by which campaign and traffic-source data is sent to Analytics and populated in reports has the following steps:

- Collection – values are sent to Google Analytics in the campaign and traffic-source fields using the SDKs or tracking code.
- Processing – collected values are used to populate the final report dimensions according to a processing logic.
- Reporting – campaign and traffic-source dimensions and metrics become available in the web interface and Reporting API.

Collection, processing, and reporting behavior can be customized.

Traffic source dimensions

Source: Every referral to a web site has an origin, or source. Possible sources include: "google" (the name of a search engine), "facebook.com" (the name of a referring site), "spring newsletter" (the name of one of your newsletters), and "direct" (users that typed your URL directly into their browser, or who had bookmarked your site).

Medium: Every referral to a website also has a medium. Possible medium include: "organic" (unpaid search), "cpc" (cost per click, i.e. paid search), "referral" (referral), "email" (the name of a custom medium you have created), "none" (direct traffic has a medium of "none").

Keyword: When SSL search is employed, Keyword will have the value *(not provided)*.

Campaign is the name of the referring Google Ads campaign or a custom campaign that you have created.

Content identifies a specific link or content item in a custom campaign. For example, if you have two call-to-action links within the same email message, you can use different Content values to differentiate them so that you can tell which version is most effective.

Personalization in PPC marketing also includes geo-targeting the ad's content and post-click landing pages to audiences in specific regions. You can use dynamic text replacement with your ads and post-click landing pages by using URL parameters of your post-click landing page to personalize the page.

Here's what using dynamic replacement text in Google Ads looks like:

For example, the dynamic replacement text in the ad above will change when a user is doing a mobile search. Mobile users will see the first ad with the text 'Free Shipping On Mobile Orders'. Users who aren't viewing the ad on a mobile device will see the second ad, which doesn't have the free shipping text on it.

The same principle is applied to post-click landing pages, where geographical locations or other content changes for different users depending on the UTM parameters you set.

Personalization in email

With email, personalization has come a long way since using the prospect's first name in the subject line and email body. First name tokens are not considered personalization anymore because it is such a common practice. Now, brands can customize automated emails with data points specific to the account.Look at Grammarly, for example. They send a weekly email with writing streak, productivity, reviewed:

Connecting every email offer with its relevant post-click landing page is one of the most basic examples of personalization. This is what Invoca does with their email and post-click landing page sequence:

A more advanced method to email personalization is inserting dynamic content in your emails to determine which recipients see each content block within the email body. Then, show them the content that you know they prefer, like Campaign Monitor allows you to do:

Personalization in marketing automation

Personalization is used in marketing automation by tailoring customer journeys to the right audience at the right time:

Effective advertising personalization encapsulates understanding users tastes and choices at a behavioral level and showing them advertising messages that you know they prefer.

While personalization and customization are two related, but different concepts, both have an impact on user experience.

Customization vs. personalization in user experience

User experience is the feeling a user has when they interact with a web page, an ad, or any other component of digital marketing. Both customization and personalization have a positive impact on user experience since they enhance the user's experience on a web page. Refer to the Netflix customized signup process earlier.

Customization improves user experience because it allows users to select their preferences, by outlining what they want, it becomes easy for marketers to show them marketing campaigns that are tailored for their specific needs.

Personalization improves user experience because marketers can create marketing campaigns based on information collected about their audience. When you know what a particular audience segment prefers, what their needs are, and what they are trying to accomplish — you can show messages that are perfectly message matched and relevant to them.

Customization vs. personalization — which is the right choice?

Instead of pinning the two approaches against each other and deciding which one to implement, use an amalgamation of both. That way, you provide your audience the best experience and marketing messages they want to see.

With customization and personalization, marketers can use multiple digital marketing channels to create optimized campaigns that users want to engage with. Review the Marketing Optimization Opportunities ebook to discover some missing opportunities you should use to increase your ROI.

Optimization of sales :

8 Ways To Optimize Sales Performance

In this section, we'll take a look at how you can optimize your sales performance by examining sales processes, communication strategy, and sales culture.

1. Establish Long-Term Goals

Every company wants to grow revenue year on year. But the only sustainable way to achieve this growth is by ignoring quick-wins and establishing long-term goals focused on quality.

The best way to achieve long-term growth is by creating the right **salesculture**. So, rather than emphasizing short-term goals like hitting monthly quotas, celebrate long-term milestones like client anniversaries or upsells.

For example, one of the core values at LinkedIn is to "act like an owner" which empowers employees to behave and make decisions as though it were their company.

This change in mindset empowers individuals to look for sustainable revenue streams instead of immediate revenue and commission:

- Low-quality revenue creates short-term value
- High-quality revenue drives long-term value

It's better to have predictable and profitable revenue streams to build long-term growth.

2. Build An Ideal Customer Profile

Building an ideal customer profile or buyer persona helps you focus on the right type of prospect. It's better to create long-term strategic relationships with ideal customers rather than chasing short-term quick wins elsewhere.

Building your buyer persona takes you past demographics and deeper into buying behaviors and emotional characteristics such as:

- Likes/Dislikes
- Buying patterns
- Motivation to purchase services and products
- Feelings and emotions that will trigger them to buy
- Common objections (and **how to handle them**)

While a buyer persona is a fictional characterization of your ideal customer, it helps to put a face to the details, like this example of "Facility Manager Fred":

SPOTIO's Sales Intelligence tool helps you create an ideal customer profile that can drive the sales prospecting process. You can **select from**

over 50 data points including income, credit capacity, the age of a home, eco-friendly, and square footage to target the best leads for your chosen territory.

3. Track and Analyze Sales Data

If you're going to optimize your sales team, then you need an effective way to track and analyze sales data.

Tracking sales leads gives your team access to metrics on what needs doing and what has already been done as part of the sales process:

You can also track sales data with Google tools.

- **Web traffic analysis** – use Google Analytics to track visitors to your website. Check which pages get the most views and leads. Conversely, check under-performing pages to see what can be improved. You can also track the most successful sources of traffic, to see where your visitors are coming from.
- **Campaign tracking** – use Google's URL Builder tool to add campaign parameters to URLs so you can track Custom Campaigns in Google Analytics.

Price optimization: Price optimization is **the process of finding the optimal price point for a product or service**. It maximizes profitability by using market and consumer data to find a balance between value and profit. Optimizing your price requires this information: Customer survey and behavior data.

Market Mix Modeling (MMM) is a technique which helps in quantifying the impact of several marketing inputs on sales or Market Share. The purpose of using MMM is to understand how much each marketing input contributes to sales, and how much to spend on each marketing input.

MMM helps in the ascertaining the effectiveness of each marketing input in terms of Return on Investment. In other words, a marketing input with higher return on Investment (ROI) is more effective as a medium than a marketing input with a lower ROI.

MMM uses the Regression technique and the analysis performed through Regression is further used for extracting key information/insights.

Market Basket Analysis: Market basket analysis is a data mining technique used by retailers to increase sales by better understanding customer purchasing patterns. It involves analyzing large data sets, such as purchase history, to reveal product groupings, as well as products that are likely to be purchased together.

The adoption of market basket analysis was aided by the advent of electronic point-of-sale (POS) systems. Compared to handwritten records kept by store owners, the digital records generated by POS systems made it easier for applications to process and analyze large volumes of purchase data.

Implementation of market basket analysis requires a background in statistics and data science, as well as some algorithmic computer programming skills. For those without the needed technical skills, commercial, off-the-shelf tools exist.

One example is the Shopping Basket Analysis tool in Microsoft Excel, which analyzes transaction data contained in a spreadsheet and performs market basket analysis. The items to be analyzed must be related by a transaction ID. The Shopping Basket Analysis tool then creates two worksheets: the Shopping Basket Item Groups worksheet, which lists items that are frequently purchased together, and the Shopping Basket Rules worksheet, which shows how items are related (For example, purchasers of Product A are likely to buy Product B).

Types of market basket analysis

There are two types of market basket analysis:

1. Predictive market basket analysis: This type considers items purchased in sequence to determine cross-sell
2. Differential market basket analysis: This type considers data across different stores, as well as purchases from different customer groups during different times of the day, month or year. If a rule holds in one

dimension (like store, time period or customer group), but does not hold in the others, analysts can determine the factors responsible for the exception. These insights can lead to new product offers that drive higher sales.

Algorithms associated with market basket analysis

In market basket analysis, association rules are used to predict the likelihood of products being purchased together. Association rules count the frequency of items that occur together, seeking to find associations that occur far more often than expected.

Algorithms that use association rules include AIS, SETM and Apriori. The Apriori algorithm is commonly cited by data scientists in research articles about market basket analysis and is used to identify frequent items in the database, then evaluate their frequency as the datasets are expanded to larger sizes.

The arules package for R is an open source toolkit for association mining using the R programming language. This package supports the Apriori algorithm, along with other mining algorithms, including arules NB Miner, opusminer, RKEEL and R Sarules.

Examples of market basket analysis

The Amazon website employs a well-known example of market basket analysis. On a product page, Amazon presents users with related products, under the headings of "Frequently bought together" and "Customers who bought this item also bought."

Market basket analysis also applies to bricks-and-mortar stores. If analysis showed that magazine purchases often include the purchase of a bookmark (which could be considered an unexpected combination, since the consumer did not purchase a book), then the book store might place a selection of bookmarks near the magazine rack.

Benefits of market basket analysis

Market basket analysis can increase sales and customer satisfaction. Using data to determine that products are often purchased together, retailers can optimize product placement, offer special deals and create new product bundles to encourage further sales of these combinations.

These improvements can generate additional sales for the retailer, while making the shopping experience more productive and valuable for customers. By using market basket analysis, customers may feel a stronger sentiment or brand loyalty toward the company.

84